On My Back, Looking Up!

On My Back, Looking Up!

To Mary & Joe
from your neighbors
John & Rose
8/85

Evelyn Orser

Review and Herald Publishing Association
Washington, DC 20039-0555
Hagerstown, MD 21740

This book was
Edited by Richard W. Coffen
Designed by Richard Steadham
Cover art by Lou Skidmore
Type set: 10/11 Optima

PRINTED IN U.S.A.

Library of Congress Cataloging in Publication Data

Orser, Evelyn, 1919-1982.
On my back, looking up!

Includes bibliographical references.
1. Multiple myeloma—Patients—United States—Biography. 2. Christian life—1960- . 3. Orser, Evelyn, 1919-1982. I. Title.
RC280.B6077 1984 362.1'96994 [B] 83-13882

ISBN 0-8280-0218-5

Dedicated

to my husband, Cecil, who has diligently cared for me,

to my wonderful mother, who has given up so much of her time and freedom to care for me, and

to our two daughters, who, in spite of living far away, have written and phoned cheery messages and have been here when possible.

My special thanks go to my dear friends Mary Casler and Barbara Atkin for the many hours they spent in helping this book become a reality. Thank-yous are also in order to all who encouraged me to write my experience, especially Pastors Phil Follett and Arvin Winkle, along with their wives, and to many more that lack of space prevents me from listing.

Contents

Foreword/9
Introduction/11
Cancer! Please, God, Say It Isn't So!/15
Searching My Way Through Science With God/23
Finding Heaven's Helpful Aids in Nature/30
Remission, With Its Hopes/37
Picking Up the Pieces/49
South of the Border/57
Growing Together Through Sharing/61
The Value of Family/64
The Big Crunch/73
Learning Through Help of Professionals/81
Home at Last!/86
Appendix/89
Epilogue/93

Foreword

Evelyn Orser is a miracle!

I first became acquainted with Evelyn when I heard of her reputation. "She is one of the most effective home Bible teachers on our staff," I was told. The secret of her success, I learned, was her intensive, earnest caring for people. She loved them, and they knew it.

Then I heard the news. Evelyn was ill. Some whispered the feared word *cancer*. We prayed that it wasn't so.

My wife and I responded when her pastor asked us to join him in praying for and anointing Evelyn. Severe pain racked her body, and she would enter the hospital within a few days for surgery. We should pray that the preliminary diagnosis of cancer was incorrect. We did. She had great faith.

The reports reached us. Evelyn did, indeed, suffer from cancer. Treatments followed. Was there remission? We continued praying.

Throughout this time, while Evelyn suffered and battled with illness, her faith grew. And the miracle continued. People who wanted to learn more about the Bible were coming to Evelyn's home, studying with her, then sharing their new experience with others. Her ministry was actually enlarging while she suffered.

We were attending a spiritual retreat in redwood country and received the bad news. Evelyn was in pain. Severe pain. We prayed for her. The next day, she was back in the hospital. But the miracle was still there. Through pain and disappointment, Evelyn's faith remained indomitable.

I heard it from a woman who stayed with her in the hospital so Evelyn's husband could get a little rest at home. I thanked the visitor for her ministry. "Oh," she replied brightly, "I count this a privilege. You don't know what a blessing it is just to be with a person who has such faith!"

A young man came to visit her. He was not particularly religious, but he valued Evelyn's friendship. He could trust her. She shared with him her faith in God. His breezy nonchalance about Heaven wavered. He sobered, tentatively testing the waters of faith in God. He wasn't quite ready to trust everything to Jesus, but he couldn't resist the loving warmth of one who knew her Lord so personally. "I'll be back again," he promised. Something had happened to him in her presence.

Was she superhuman? No. Sometimes she became discouraged. Sometimes she was just plain tired. But always she had a firm, genuine confidence that God is good and that she could trust Him. Even when doubts crowded her mind, her heart clung to Him.

I believe in miracles. I believe God can and does heal. I also believe in miracles when, in the midst of suffering, people who love life cry out from between quivering lips, "I know that God is love."

This book is Evelyn's testimony about her confidence in Jesus. Her faith is a miracle. And I believe in miracles.

Philip Follett

Introduction

For nearly four years now you've been looking on while a dread disease has been taking its ugly toll within the frame of someone you care about. You've prayed. You've shed some tears. You've held on to your faith as best you've known how. You've asked "Why?" Sometimes you've even read the counsel to "think it not strange concerning the fiery trial which is to try you . . . but rejoice" (1 Peter 4:12, 13).

You've offered material help and counsel. You've shared the latest news on cancer cures. You've made every effort to show your love and concern. You've spent precious time and money and gasoline to ease the difficult journeys for treatment day after day. You've sent delicious food to the home. Beautiful flowers have scented the house while the patient could still appreciate their fragrance and beauty. Many are the cheerful and happy phone calls you've made. You've laughed and shared the fun things going on—not the morbid!

Down deep inside, your questions have been many. "Why, God? We've prayed for healing. Is this Your answer—No? Will You heal even yet? Couldn't this have happened to one of the derelicts who has no concern for You? Are You punishing? How can *good* come out of this?"

You also may be facing possible death, and you are very young. You've helped your friend many times, but you're not sure about this God she trusts so much. Because you are not too well acquainted with Him, you're just a little afraid to let go and let Him have complete control. Many, many unanswered questions keep spinning around in your head.

You may belong to the little family that has shared a lot of love and already lost some very precious ones in the valley of the shadow of death. You've adopted as your own the one who suffers—long before you knew this would happen. Have you ever almost wished you had never cared this much? Never come to know this one, now to hurt because she hurts?

Perhaps you treated the afflicted one in therapy. You really didn't want that patient in the first place when you learned the nature of the disease. Why should you put yourself through that hurt again? Hadn't God already done enough when He struck down two of your own loved ones with the same disease? (We sometimes blame God for something that is not His fault.) But you were assigned the patient, and you had no choice. (You don't tell the boss you will not give therapy to this patient!) You and the patient become good friends—and more questions pounded into your brain. "If God is love, why? Why? Why?"

You may be a person who is trying to hang on to God. You know He's up there, yet because of hypocrites in the church, you feel you can be nearer to Him by separating yourself from the fellowship. Who needs fellowship with those who have dealt dishonestly in business? Maybe you, like some of the rest of us, have been hurt by such individuals. You have concluded that it's better to stay on the outside and look in. You aren't exactly comfortable out there, either, but it's better than being one of them. Now one you really love is hanging on in constant pain. What good is it to stay on the inside only to suffer like this? If God is really up there, why doesn't He *do* something?

Or possibly you have much faith. You believe that if you trust and believe *enough,* God will heal this special person. You encourage her to *really* believe that she is healed—and she will be. You yourself conjure up in your own heart an added amount of this elusive entity called faith and just *know* the answer is already there.

The questions tumble around faster than the answers come. These queries and many more have pounded the temples of the one who for these four years has been living with multiple myeloma, a type of bone cancer.

I am this person.

To each of you I address this book, because as I have tried to search out the answers, our heavenly Father has tucked me in with such a blanket of blessings that I feel compelled to share them.

As I share with you some of the fears, pains, hopes, yet most of all the heavenly gifts we call blessings, it is with the prayer that some of your questions may turn into quests for truth—the truly healing kind that a loving heavenly Father so very much wants you to experience.

I must confess that all the answers are not clear to me yet, but His love has come through in such abundance that I would choose no other way than His. You see, eternity is so near that the things of earth have grown strangely dim in the light of His glory and grace.

Cancer! Please, God, Say It Isn't So!

All evidence points to multiple myeloma. See these hot spots on your spinal X-rays?" The orthopedic specialist, a personal friend, measured his words carefully as he pointed out the diseased areas that were clearly defined on the X-ray film. Then slowly, almost painfully, he turned to face me.

"And what is myeloma?" I asked.

"Evelyn, it's cancer. Bone cancer!"

The words thundered over me like an ocean wave—overpowering, cold, foreboding! I tried to voice my words calmly: "What would you do, Doctor, if you were me?" He offered some suggestions, double-checked on the last scan, and reported that the radiologist still was questioning the reports, so we would have to check further to know for sure. However, he had no doubts.

Limp deep within from the impact of his findings, yet calm and collected on the surface, I made my way from his office out to the street. I turned my footsteps toward home, a half block away. "Lord," I breathed, "this can't be! It must be a dream. Not me! How many times have I thanked You for the good health You have given me? How many times have I smiled inwardly as people have commented, 'You must really live right! You're always so healthy!' " Their words expressed a suggestion that caressed my ego. Sure! I *am* healthy, and yes, I *do* live right, and God blesses me for it!

I kicked at a shriveled leaf lying on the sidewalk. Dead leaves. Death. Maybe this is it for me soon, too! Poor little leaf!

One season was its full allotment. I had enjoyed fifty-eight years of life at its fullest. Even though gray-white hair had replaced the brown hair of years back, I still held my head high and took pride in my personal appearance. The gray hair had turned out better than the brown when it came to colors I could wear. Yes, I rather liked the change, even with the added years that came with it.

My life overflowed with so many worthwhile fun things. Besides teaching Bible, I served as a volunteer at the hospital as well and was deeply involved in other community activities. Having spent thirteen years in business, I had learned to meet the public comfortably. Life was worthwhile!

My marriage to Cecil had always been happy—one that never lacked for surprises and new interests. This 5′ 10″ of real man in my life was no passive personality. He was impetuous and sometimes explosive, yet beneath all the rumbles, he was truly a quiet, loving, easy-going type. That may sound contradictory, but such is the person I married and love. We both often admitted openly that of all the problems we each might have, marital problems were not among them.

And the girls! Pat, the older one, was a calm, smiling girl who always cooperated and seemed ever to hold the best interests of others ahead of her own. She had always remained sensitive to our needs—always ready to carry her share of the load. Now she mothered two small children of her own. How we missed her and loved the times we could get together with her and her family. If only she didn't live way across the continent!

Beth was the younger—vivacious, fun loving, happy, and always running, with her French braids flying in the air as she went! She was now the mother of three little ones and lived in Iowa. Sometimes I could hardly bear having them so far away. The times spent in their little home were special, too, as from year to year we visited them.

This was our family, and now I must tell them the bad news. How could I do it? How would Cec react? I knew of cases in which the mates couldn't handle such news and after a while gave up the marriage—but, no, that wasn't my Cec. What about the girls? Could they understand and hold up with wanting to rush to my side? Were they mature enough? I'd never prepared them for anything like this.

Another leaf caught under my toe as I shuffled homeward. Why should I get cancer, anyway? Mom was healthy and in her late 70s. Dad had no cancer, and he was nearly 86. No one among my many brothers and sisters were ill with anything. All were married happily to their original spouses. But Grandpa had died of cancer. He was so far away at the time that I hadn't realized the seriousness of his problem.

I kicked the leaf aside and pondered: This couldn't be *me!* But it *was* me, and I was a seriously ill person—just beginning the pathway traveled by many before me, the pathway leading through a tumultuous battle to live; just beginning to learn from a loving heavenly Father about the many ways His love would manifest itself even through pain and illness.

Had I known in advance of the multitude of times I would have to recite my history to each department, doctor, or specialist, and of the many tests—some simple, some painful, some tedious—my courage might have dipped into depression. Yet, true to His promises, our all-knowing God reminded me through His Word that "there hath no temptation taken you but such as is common to man: but God is faithful, who will not suffer you to be tempted above that ye are able; but will with the temptation also make a way to escape, that ye may be able to bear it" (1 Cor. 10:13). Impossible as it may seem, surprising even to me, the fears began to lift until each encounter became another challenge I could take to Him. Each time, He would give me the solace and the strength to face another crisis.

Sufficient evidence for a definite diagnosis was lacking those first months. Spinal needle biopsy, bone marrow, blood tests—none were conclusive.

Time was the next factor I had to deal with. Time was a blessing and a curse, because with it came moments of blissful hope that it could all be a mistaken conclusion. I found myself retreating deep into this fantasy. It was so comfortable there! Time also brought moments of fear, horrible dread, that reminded me over and over to grasp God's promises and hang on.

Books about cancer and cancer cures invited me to try numerous methods of healing. A few friends suggested faith healers, just in case the tests should confirm cancer. Some urged going to a foreign land to meet with a "great healer." My study of Scripture through the years had led me to the realization that even the devil can perform miracles. If I were to seek out a "healer," he must certainly, beyond a doubt, employ scriptural methods. "To the law and to the testimony: If they speak not according to this word, it is because there is no light in them" (Isa. 8:20). The divine Healer gave us some specifics in James 5.

I struggled with how best to explain this conviction to an earnest friend who deeply desired my healing. Did the healer she had heard of follow the Bible injunction? In my own heart I had decided that I would rather die than be healed by the devil. It did not then occur to me how soon I would have to decide whether or not to follow only the Biblical counsel.

Seven months passed quickly. The doctors decided to do a surgical biopsy in my rib cage. Because we had planned to attend a ten-day church retreat, it was decided the surgery would take place when we returned. By this time spasmodic pain in the ribs had begun to trouble me.

We headed north for our highly anticipated vacation. We camped in a wooded area near a river and enjoyed the music and messages from God's holy Word. In addition to sitting and listening, my husband and I walked for miles along a railroad track. We found a large patch of blackberry bushes. The fruit was so delicious we just had to return with car and containers and pick enough for a big berry cobbler. During our hike and as I reached far into the bushes for the berries, the pain in my ribs became more persistent. By nightfall the pain demanded total quiet and rest.

The final weekend of the retreat was approaching. Now and

then, as the pain would temporarily ease up, I would slip into a chair at the meeting and drink in all I could of the messages given.

The closing church service was in session. As long as I sat still, the pain was bearable, so it seemed as good to be taking in the service as to stay in camp. The minister ended his remarks, and the outdoor congregation sang a final hymn. Knowing full well the change of position would make rising from the chair most difficult, I purposely waited for Cecil to look the other way. I didn't want him to be alarmed by the pain reflected on my face. The moment came; wincing with pain, I struggled to my feet. In my concentrated effort, I failed to notice my pastor standing nearby, observing the battle I was having.

Sidling nearer, he commented, "You're in pain!" There was no denying it. Cecil turned back from greeting a friend on his other side just as the pastor asked, "Have you considered requesting special prayer and anointing?" Yes, I had seriously considered it.

After a short discussion, we concluded that I would pray about it while I searched my own heart and asked for guidance. To me this would be a very solemn request to make of God. I would be asking the King of the universe, the Creator of all things, to restore me to health. Could I, in turn, totally give my all to Him in a renewed commitment?

My decision came quickly after I had asked God to be my strength and my fortress in the times ahead and to forgive me for my failures in the past. "Is any sick among you? let him call for the elders of the church; and let them pray over him, anointing him with oil in the name of the Lord" (James 5:14). The elders met with us that very afternoon. Three ministers pleaded earnestly for the power of Heaven to heal me, according to the will of God.

As they read excerpts from Scripture, my faith was strengthened to recognize that God answers such requests in various ways. Some people find immediate, complete recovery. For others the experience is gradual. Still others will not find healing until the day our Lord returns when all who have chosen Him will be changed in "the twinkling of an eye" to immortal health (1 Cor. 15:52).

Of course, deep inside I longed for the immediate answer, but I saw no bright flash of light nor felt an electric shock—just a quiet, still, small Voice that spoke of trust and my willingness to allow our heavenly Father to take charge as He saw fit.

Soberly, yet, oh, so peacefully, we returned to camp. A small group of friends had gathered nearby to add their prayers. As I lay quietly on the camper bed that night, texts flashed into my mind that brought confidence and added faith. "I will never leave thee, nor forsake thee" (Heb. 13:5). "Thou wilt keep him in perfect peace, whose mind is stayed on thee" (Isa. 26:3). "Bless the Lord, O my soul, and forget not all his benefits: who forgiveth all thine iniquities; who healeth all thy diseases" (Ps. 103:2, 3).

The next day, as we headed for home, these and other promises gently permeated my thoughts. They reminded me that I would not walk this road alone. The three-hour journey over, home looked good! Cecil set about to unload the camping equipment. I found my way to the couch and tried not to worry him with the pain that wracked my body.

Bewildering thoughts chased one another in circles. God, is it not best that I should be healed completely of this pain? I guess, Lord, I must admit to being a bit disappointed that the pain didn't go away immediately yesterday. Hang on to me, Lord! My own ability to hang on is weak just now.

After this brief conversation with God, I started to get up from the couch. I wanted to help Cecil put things away in the cupboards. But pain grabbed me severely, so I rolled over and slid my knees to the floor. I figured that from this position I could stagger to my feet. But I could not pull myself up. My husband entered the room, took one startled look, helped me back to the couch, and immediately called the doctor.

The next day I entered the hospital for surgery. The physicians zeroed in on a tumor infesting a rib. They removed it and sent it out for analysis.

As I began to regain consciousness, I naturally asked

myself, "Is it really myeloma—for sure?" Becoming aware that someone was checking my incision, I opened my eyes and found the surgeon standing beside me. "Is it true, Doctor?" He seemed not to hear me. "Doctor, is it really cancer?" His lips tightened as he seemed totally preoccupied with his task of checking my bandages. I thought I saw him nod his head in answer. Realizing that he was the surgeon and not the attending physician, I felt perhaps he would prefer not to convey any news to the patient. Besides, the pathology report would provide the final verdict. I dropped the subject.

With the removal of the tumor, the pain disappeared, and life seemed rosy once again. Friends came in and out. One day passed, then two. Evening came. Lights were dimmed after visiting hours. My husband had left for home. All was quiet.

A light knock on the door broke the stillness. My family doctor and the orthopedic specialist slipped into the room. If they had never verbalized their message, it still would have been there as they searched for words to make the news easier for me to handle. Again, I did not cry. I recognized that I must face what had already appeared probable. Yet the shock sank deep into my consciousness as we talked of future treatments and possibilities.

The men left. I was about to struggle through the way I usually preferred—alone with God, but the door opened quietly. Suddenly a tall figure stood beside the bed. Like an angel sent for this moment, my pastor was there to join me in prayer. Once again my heavenly Father was reminding me that I was not alone.

At home, half a block away, my husband was sleeping, unaware of the trauma I was enduring. But he was in my room early the next day to check on my welfare during the night. Since he worked at the hospital, he had only to walk down the hall to begin the day's work. He had not seen the doctors or the pastor, so he was not quite prepared for the news, "The diagnosis *is* cancer—multiple myeloma."

We were so brave for each other! I broke the news to him gently, matter-of-factly; after all, we knew it could be cancer.

He listened in stoic silence, holding my hand. No tears. I felt then that I must protect him from so much hurt and that he would be brave for my sake.

Protecting each other from the hurt of reality seemed very necessary to both of us as we stood at the threshold of a whole new experience. Neither of us found it easy to discuss the future. Avoiding reference even to the word *cancer* seemed most comfortable. Whether or not we were denying the inevitable was unimportant at that point. We did and said the things that had to be done and said in deciding which way to turn for help. Through it all we stayed close, even though we suppressed conversation concerning our specific feelings and fears. Praying together, as we had always done, brought solace, strength, and a growing closeness to God that sustained us in spite of our fears.

In a few days the doctors released me from the hospital. Despite the ominous prognosis, I felt little pain. Hope for possible remission surged through me. I relished being home again, buoyed up by friends who stopped by to chat, and my family, who phoned often. How good God is!

But what of the future? Was my work for God over? Have You grounded me, Lord? I speculated. Fighting for my own life, how would I ever be able to help my community, my church family, or my immediate family? Was there anything left that I could do? His answer came through to me as I searched His letter—His Word—again. "I am the Lord thy God which teacheth thee to profit, which leadeth thee by the way that thou shouldest go" (Isa. 48:17). He reminded me again of His injunction, "Follow me, and I will make you fishers of men" (Matt. 4:19). "Ye shall be witnesses unto me" (Acts 1:8).

I found no word excusing me from continuing to witness for Him, no matter what my future held. Could it be that I might yet find opportunities to tell others about His great love? Could my personal battle between life and death speak to others of God's mighty power and of His concern for His children on Planet Earth?

Searching My Way Through Science With God

With every new phase in our lives there come adjustments—from babyhood through childhood, into adolescence and adulthood. The thought had occurred to me several times in recent years: Well, I've made it through all but retirement. That will be next!

But it was not next.

I had not planned for a period in which I must deal with a terminal illness. Having weathered the initial shock of realizing the seriousness of this new phase and experiencing the satisfaction of total dependence on God for every day that dawned, I now could look ahead with a positive attitude. He is the blessed Controller of all things. Miraculously, my fears left me. Contentment, happiness, and joy filled my life more than ever before.

But soon a renewed deluge of questions from friends rained upon me. Some of the questions I had also asked. Some, I believe, may not be answered until we see Him face to face. I entered a time of deep searching, but it was also a time of sharing.

Suddenly I became aware of all the others who were also suffering from cancer. Through my volunteer work at the hospital, I received invitations to meet patients. Together we shared our experiences, and it opened many opportunities to lift these people before God, praying for His love and care to comfort them. Some of them, already trusting in His grace, enriched my life by sharing with me the beautiful thoughts that they had gained during their ordeal.

One day I quietly slipped into a room and found a very despondent gentleman sitting up in his bed. He had totally tuned out the world. I greeted him cheerfully, hoping for a response. He looked up, grunted, and with a tremor in his voice said, "I just found out I have cancer!" He might have added, "And that's all I'm going to say, so please go away!"

I hesitated, then out it came: "I'm sorry! I have cancer, too. I think I can understand how you feel."

His face jerked as he turned to look at me. "You have it, too?" And he was able to open up and talk about his fears and needs.

Quite soon after I learned I had cancer I discovered that cancer sufferers choose between two ways of coping. Many bury the thought that they have cancer. They do not use the word *cancer* in their conversation, as at first I did not, but refer only to their "illness." They do not care to be around when the topic is discussed. Thus they block from their minds what they cannot face. Others freely discuss the matter. They ask questions. They join informational groups for help in understanding their plight. They seek out methods to fight the malignancy.

In my observations, the latter group seemed much better prepared to make more intelligent choices, so I chose that route. The choice has been most rewarding! Yes, it has aroused feelings of anger at times, because when people talk so openly, they sometimes unintentionally say things that strike a sensitive chord within. However, talking freely has quite often instigated some humor, and that, for me, has been a lifesaver. When Solomon wrote, "A merry heart doeth good like a medicine," I think he included good humor, for even during my darkest moments, seeing the humorous side has been of much value.

A classic example came when an older doctor friend who hadn't seen me for a while looked dolefully at me and said, "Well, Evelyn, we all have to die sometime!"

My first reaction was, "Don't say that!" but instantly the humor of it surfaced, and I chuckled to myself as I walked away. (Throughout these chapters bits of the fun side will filter in, not because I want to sound flippant, but to describe another of Heaven's blessings that helped me handle what otherwise would have seemed to be an impossible situation.)

Time at home was very brief after my short hospital stay. As soon as possible, I needed to check with two more specialists. Radiation and chemotherapy were alternative methods for treating myeloma.

Indeed, all the fears that had ever crossed my mind concerning the use of such hazardous means of treatment surfaced at this time. Having owned and managed a health-food store for thirteen years, I had sold many books on cancer cures. I desperately wanted to go the "natural" route. On the other hand, my close association with the medical profession also helped me realize my need for all the scientific aid possible. Should I cut myself off from this source? If so, what then? No, I needed my doctors, and even some of them encouraged as much of the "natural" methods as possible. My husband and I conferred and decided to see both specialists, hear their counsel, and pray for God's guidance in making a decision.

Once again I faced batteries of questions as these dedicated men probed for every detail of my case history. They studied carefully the X-rays and scans. Both my husband and I appreciated the radiology oncologist's simple explanations. By use of a powerful machine, this doctor explained, the diseased area would be treated by "linear acceleration," whereby the specific area of disease would receive radiation. This would be done in a series of thirteen treatments. Each treatment would last about one minute.

As he reviewed the nuclear scans and X-rays, he found that two or three hot spots which were on the film six months previously were not visible on the present X-rays. The doctor hummed a note or two, then, looking at me, he exclaimed, "Hmmm! You have something going for you! These spots disappeared, even without treatment!"

"Thank You, Lord!" Whatever was "going for me" had its source with Him. This was exciting news to hear!

"Now," said the doctor, "we're ready to start. There's an area on your upper spine that is a hot one. We should treat it quickly. Shall we go ahead? I can advise, but you must make the final decision."

Now what? If I waited, would this spot also heal? Or would it enlarge and grow? How could I know? A silent message sped heavenward: "Dear Lord, please guide us in our choices. We're having to decide this one so fast!" Cecil and I pondered a bit, groping for an answer, then I decided to move ahead with the treatment.

My thoughts raced ahead as they prepared me for the first treatment. A pleasant young woman ushered me into a dressing room and instructed me to put on a wrap-around gown. While I sat wondering what would happen next, and feeling anything but ready for a photographer, a young man with a camera appeared from somewhere and took my picture. No permission, no anything! After another short wait I wound up in a room that resembled an X-ray room. A huge machine occupied most of the space. Another young man asked me to climb onto the table, face down, and as I did so, the photographer reappeared and snapped a picture of my back. The technicians and the doctor then conferred and with colored pens drew lines on my back, marking off the area to be radiated. Next, with careful precision, they designated the exact spot by tattooing permanently a mark that would forever indicate the treated place. They adjusted the large overhead equipment so that it pointed just to the marked spot. Inside I quivered in fear, but I tried to remind myself that God had sent His angels to stand beside me.

After they told me to lie very still, the technicians all left the room. The big door closed. I was alone! A buzzing sound began. Would it zap me out of existence? No! I had seen people coming out of these rooms. They had walked out and seemed unafraid. The buzzing stopped, and the technicians returned, announcing that it was all over until the next treatment. Whew! And I didn't feel a thing! When I climbed down from the table, I was relieved to realize that I, too, could walk from the room. Thus began the first of a series of radiation treatments.

My home doctor had urged me to meet with the oncologist, the specialist who treats cancer with chemotherapy. I had some real fears of chemotherapy, so as we conferred with this man I laid bare my soul in explaining them to him. He listened attentively, explained carefully the values of chemotherapy, and told me that usually chemotherapy and radiation were not used simultaneously. With the radiation series already begun, he would advise oral chemotherapy.

Because of my questions the doctor also advised a second opinion. Following his advice, we spent a day with doctors at Stanford University Hospital. Their diagnosis reiterated the original findings, and they advised oral chemotherapy. Pointedly the specialist at Stanford said to me, "Don't allow anyone to give you more than the oral. If the oral isn't successful, any further chemotherapy would do you no good!"

It had been a long day, and my strength was at a low ebb. We stopped to rest a bit in the city where we had previously agreed to meet a brother and his wife at a motel. I suppose that I had faintly hoped that these doctors would write off all the former reports. Now I knew this could not be.

Soon after returning home I again checked in with the oncologist. The radiation treatments were nearing completion. Arrangements were made for oral chemotherapy. My reservations about this route still left me highly dubious, yet I was eager to use every method that could possibly bring remission.

One month passed with no significant changes in my feelings of well-being. My face glowed with a ruddy appearance and took on the full-moon shape that often accompanies the ingestion of prednisone. The oncologist kept a careful check through blood tests, urine analyses, and frequent personal interviews. At the end of one month he seemed disappointed with his conclusions, and explained that so far I had not responded to treatment. Another month passed with a similar report. At the end of three months he sighed—still no results! He thought perhaps we should move on to stronger dosages. Stronger dosages? My mind went into a tailspin. The words of the Stanford doctor echoed in my mind: "Don't allow . . . more than the oral."

The seriousness and concern on the face of my oncologist sitting at his desk before me betrayed his anxiety. We discussed the report from Stanford, which he had in his files. Abruptly he stood and left the room. I sat on the edge of the examining table as I awaited his return. An eternity passed. The nurse stepped in to assure me that the doctor would soon return.

When he reentered the room, he brought a thick book, which he explained he had just received. It listed treatments given by university hospitals around the United States for many kinds of cancer. It was the latest report. He carefully studied the reports and treatments given particularly for myeloma, concluding that the dosage was conservative as compared with those used for many other types of cancer. Hence, he would not administer the heavier dosages. Looking at me, he asked, "What do you want to do? I'll gladly back you, send you wherever you might like to go, as long as it is conventional medicine." Bless him! "As long as it is conventional . . ."

That's what I had been receiving—conventional therapy and radiation. And, in fact, I had received further radiation when a tumor had formed on my sternum, had grown and then had fractured. It had produced almost instant pain of such intensity that within a few minutes I was prostrate on the couch and gasping for breath.

With radiation treatments the pain soon subsided and within two months an X-ray showed new bone growth already filling in. As the radiologist pointed this out to me, my courage rose again, even though I knew I must remember that tumors might develop in other bone areas.

Yes, conventional medicine had helped greatly. I was also interested in learning more about how diet, exercise, water, and fresh air could be used in natural therapy. It seemed reasonable to me to provide any possible aid for the immune system.

My mind had been toying with trying an organization run

by conventional doctors who had stepped aside from their affluent practices and had opened a health-conditioning center. It was located some 175 miles from us, and though newly established, it had already obtained noticeable attention. After a twenty-six-day stay, their guests left with much improved health. Could I benefit from trying their program? Did I dare mention this to the concerned doctor sitting before me? Yes, I would!

As I described the center to the specialist, I bore down on the fact that one of the doctors was an internal medicine specialist. He shook his head. "I can't back you in this. I've never heard of the place."

I couldn't blame him for that, but asked, "Would you send my records if I decide to go?" Yes, he would do that. Then, expressing my strong desire to try a twenty-six-day session, I thanked him for his care and asked that I might return for a checkup later on. He kindly agreed.

A brand-new venture was about to begin.

Finding Heaven's Helpful Aids in Nature

Weimar Institute'' the sign announced, as my husband, his mother, and I entered the gates of what would be my home for nearly a month. After I had checked in and rested an hour or so, my family said their goodbyes and slowly drove away, heading back home. I watched the car vanish from sight, and a lump formed in my throat. ''I feel institutionalized!'' I groaned to myself. But this was no time for self-pity. This choice was my own, and now was the time to begin!

Back at my room I quickly finished unpacking. The meager little cell, once a nurses' station in a TB ward, began to take on the appearance of a dormitory room. The bed was comfortable. Clean linen was in readiness. And this was Room 13!

Soon the whole group would convene for the first meeting. Meanwhile, some were checking in and others strolled around the beautiful grounds, resplendent with tall pine trees, madrone, manzanita—all of it much as Mother Nature had planted it. A few lonely little flowers hung their heads as they prepared to sleep through the rest of the winter. It was January in California.

Warm inside my puffy jacket, I ventured down a beckoning pathway. In the distance I could see a long hothouse, where many young plants were nurtured. Here and there I noticed curious-looking houses—some stark and abandoned, some bright with ruffled curtains peeping from behind an unpainted exterior.

Now and then I met other people. There were joggers and

strollers. Some seemed bent on reaching a destination. Others appeared to be curious, as I was. Later I concluded that all strollers were newcomers. After a day or two of walks, and lectures on proper exercise, all the guests moved as if they were going somewhere!

Supper would be served at six o'clock, and an orientation was to follow. As we gathered in the warmth of the cafeteria with its big old wood-burning heater, I little realized that this room full of tables and chairs and checkered plastic tablecloths would be transformed into a cozy place to sit and chat when day was done. Here people from faraway places and near; from rich homes and poor would blend together. Here we would share and share alike, and within twenty-six days would gain many lifetime friends.

They had come from Canada, Kansas, Washington, D.C., and Oregon as well as from nearby places in California. A handsome couple who sat across the table from me especially attracted my attention. She looked the part of a model. Long, flowing blonde hair tumbled gracefully around her face and shoulders. He, the Clark Gable type, was obviously a successful man of the world. He was tall and had graying temples and mustache. "Wonder which one is the patient?" I mused. They both looked too good to be true!

The entrance of two smiling young ladies carrying food to the serving table interrupted my thoughts. Immediately all eyes aimed in the same direction. What would we have for our first meal at Weimar? Warm applesauce over toast. No cream or whipped cream to add a bit of zest to it. Then there were fresh bananas and oranges. That was it! The girls served us in such a happy manner that any dampened spirits over the menu were swallowed up in delightful conversation.

In the Weimar classroom throughout the next few days we learned, among other things, that

1. The immune system handles getting rid of germs.

2. The immune system recognizes cancer cells and will go after them.

3. As we grow older, the immune system tends to break

down and does not always keep up in the battle.

4. Certain drugs tend to suppress the immune system.

We also learned that white blood cells are involved in the immune system. The lecturer explained that there are different kinds of white blood cells:

1. *Neutrophils*—the kind that engulf bacteria and then digest them through the action of enzymes found in little sacs called *lysosomes*.

2. *Lymphocytes*—these recognize foreign proteins (bacteria, viruses, cancer cells) and destroy them through complex mechanisms involving the immune globulins, interferon, and other factors.

Sunshine and heat can stimulate the activity of the white blood cells.

By eating refined foods we inhibit our immune system. It was reported that one teaspoon of sugar undermines the ability of the cells to engulf or kill germs. A banana split could freeze their ability to function. This is why we saw no sugar anywhere.

Early the next morning we were whisked away in carloads to a doctor's office in nearby Auburn. We spent most of the day there having blood tests, EKGs, and treadmill tests. No breakfast before these tests. Fruit would be the only fare for this particular day.

Byron, a tall, healthy specimen of a young man, and, appropriately enough, the head of the physical therapy department, talked to the group. He acquainted us with the campus and oriented us to our new surroundings.

Suppertime came—more fruit! Bob, across from me, groaned. He cast a disdainful glance at the serving table and muttered, "I don't think I can take this!"

"Shhh!" warned his pretty wife.

With food as the topic, a conversation was not difficult to launch. Besides, this motley little group had sat most of the day staring at each other in the reception room at the doctor's office. We had begun to feel acquainted. Bob spoke again. This time he addressed those of us nearest to him. "You see, I'm a meat-and-potatoes man! Smoked cigarettes all the time and always had my drinks. Knew that had to go if I came here, but I'm just not sure I can hack this food!" And with this he punctuated his remarks by adding, "And I sure do want a cigarette!" As though understanding that a morale builder would come in handy about now, a staff member sauntered into the room, backed up to the warmth of the crackling fire, glanced around the room as though he couldn't wait to get to know each of us, smiled, and introduced himself.

He was John, chaplain of the reconditioning center. Across the table Bob ducked his head, "What now! Some religion, I suppose!" John introduced us to some fun-type singing. Some in two parts, some in rounds. Usually the songs were Scriptures set to music. At first all we heard was John's rich bass voice, but one by one we caught on until the room was echoing with praises to God. Bob and Joyce were singing lustily, enjoying every minute of it. That's how day one came to an end.

Tuesday morning breakfast at 6:45 brought steamed whole-grain cereal (no milk), toast of homemade bread (no butter), and an orange. The cereal was passable, but cooked without salt. The shakers on the tables might have helped, but closer investigation revealed that they contained onion and garlic powder. No, thanks! After another short and happy few minutes of singing with John, we were introduced to our first medical lecture. A doctor from a nearby city, who had himself suffered heart problems and a stroke, told of his own experience and of the value that a similar program had been to him. He lectured further on diet and exercise and their importance to our bodies.

Nine-thirty meant calisthenics with Byron. I could hear plenty of huffing and puffing, grunting and groaning, as tight muscles were stretched beyond their usual capacity. My first appointment with a medical person was lined up for this second day of our new venture. I had been assigned to see the internist of the staff on a regular weekly basis for the duration of the program. Hurrying to her office, I wondered, Now what? As the doctor beckoned me into the examining room, her warm smile and unassuming air put me at ease immediately.

She had seen my X-rays and medical reports. "Your X-rays show the right-shoulder-blade area to be badly chewed up," she commented. Then she turned my thoughts to God and His healing power, explaining that the procedure being used at Weimar was one of doing all possible to cooperate with God's plan for the care of our bodies, then asking His blessing and healing. There, in her modest little office, she prayed that God would take charge and guide in the care that I would receive. The love and concern already shown by everyone on the staff moved me. Now it unfolded day after day as each technician, nurse, or student spent time with me. On walks, in treatment, or just in simple chats, the same love of God repeatedly came through. Nearly everyone who spent time with me offered a prayer. I knew that the other fourteen guests who shared this program also received the same personal attention.

God's love was so real that we responded spontaneously, though our group included Christians and non-Christians. Even Bob was warming up, and a gentleness softened his usual matter-of-factness. His set jaw relaxed into a pleasant smile as the power of this love infiltrated his inner being. The whole group began to become as a family unit.

At mealtime we became free with our questions: "Why not a little salt? Why no butter? Do we ever get to have milk? Why garlic powder in the saltshakers?" One by one the answers came. The young ladies had heard many of these questions from previous guests.

They explained that within a few days our appetites would change. What seemed saltless and sometimes tasteless would soon begin to taste good. The majority of guests were taking this course owing to heart disease, overweight, or vascular problems. For all the guests the staff had chosen a "therapeutic" diet, which, though spectacularly different from a usual diet, succeeded in effecting some rather remarkable changes within a short period of time. No added salt was part of this careful diet. The shakers containing onion or garlic powder were for those with a compulsion to dash something on their food before eating.

No visible fats, another no-no, knocked a lot of my favorite foods down the drain. However, it was no longer a shock. One of the lectures dealt with fats. I was appalled and preferred to deny the facts brought out by the physician. Yet, because this man was about to receive his doctorate in the field of nutrition at a nearby renowned university, it did seem reasonable to hear him through. I had used a lot of unsaturated fats, being confident for some years that so long as the fat was in liquid form and from a vegetable source I was safe. Now I heard about some recent discoveries concerning fats in various forms and the need to minimize using any of them.

The fats found in their natural state—as in nuts, avocados, and olives—were good foods if used in moderation. In the therapeutic diet, even these seldom appeared on our tables, and we were learning in cooking class how to prepare foods without using the free fats. Soon the aromas and appearance of delicious foods prepared by the happy kitchen crew delighted us. Our daily exercise and the absence of between-meal snacks had whetted our appetites.

Spinach lasagne was made without cheese. Great varieties of fresh and steamed vegetables were served. Whole-grain muffins and breads, without butter, were served with spreads made by blending softened dried fruits. Other spreads were made of mashed garbanzos mixed with tasty ingredients. We enjoyed cornbread made with no sugar or baking powder, which afforded us opportunity to learn other methods of causing the cornbread to rise. The light evening meal consisted mostly of fruits and toast or bread. It became my favorite meal of the day.

About a week after our arrival, several of us came to the happy conclusion that as time progressed the cooks were fixing more tasty meals. Bob and Joyce revealed our conversation to the girls as they served us that evening. With a twinkle in their eyes the cooks thanked us and then reminded us that a good part of the change, as they had predicted, had taken place in our own taste buds.

The remainder of our twenty-six-day stay at Weimar was

routine now: good food, hikes, sunbathing, calisthenics, reminders to drink lots of water, counsel to ask Heaven's guidance, and counsel to trust in God's unlimited power. The more we talked of it and sang of it, the easier we found it to believe. Using the very elements God in His mercy had provided for our well-being and recognizing His healing power at work within the framework of His original plan, we thrilled in anticipation of what our closer cooperation with Him might reveal to each of us individually.

Our final evening together had come. Rumors had spilled out that we would have a very special supper that night. Our spouses were invited to join us if they had not already been there throughout the program. As we entered the dining room, a festive sight met our eyes. Beautifully decorated tables, shimmering in candlelight, beckoned us to our designated places. Centerpieces made artistically from melons, strawberries, pineapples, bananas, apples, and oranges delighted our eyes, evoking more than one expression of appreciation from the guests.

The meal and the program were a memorable occasion, filled with happy songs, a bit of humor, and words of encouragement from the staff. Twenty-six days had come and gone so fast! Departure on the morrow would mean separation forever from this special group that had become like a family. Outside, a heavy snow was blanketing the landscape, turning it into a wonder world of white.

Tomorrow we would travel homeward. Back to the reality of preparing our own food. Back to waiting upon instead of being waited on. Yet back to a life that would be changed somewhat from what it had been before. "Really," I mused, "what *is* ahead for me?"

Remission, With Its Hopes

Six weeks had hurried by before I made another appointment with my oncologist. He ordered X-rays to check on the hot spot areas and asked for blood and urine tests. The reports revealed one tiny affected area, and he asked if I would undergo a second series of chemotherapy.

Since the tests showed such a marked improvement, I decided not to undergo further chemotherapy at that time. I did not rule out the possibility that later I might reverse my decision, but it seemed worth a try now to see whether the few cancer cells in evidence would also disappear if I continued to live by the principles I had learned so recently.

A few months later the physician called for additional marrow tests, and I had the thrill of hearing the word *remission*. I felt sure that the natural program had truly helped me.

When warm days arrived I took up sunbathing out on the patio. Each day began early as I took a vigorous walk in the company of several exercise enthusiasts. Life took on a rosy glow. Hopes soared.

Not satisfied to enjoy such happiness by myself, I resumed an active life of teaching. For some years, sharing the beauty of God's Word with others had been my work. I gave studies on a one-to-one basis in private homes or in our home, wherever the schedule best fitted. Some studies were conducted in groups if the students preferred it that way. My chief aim was to help others gain an interest in searching the Scriptures, thus finding satisfactory answers to their questions. More important than knowledge, however, was the need for the students to come to know God Himself in a personal way. In so doing they would experience the abundant life He promised in John 10:10, "I am come that they might have life, and that they might have it more abundantly." It seemed almost a compulsion within me to become involved again in this work.

Finally, I had set up several appointments for new studies. Each one brought the thrill of a new friend and a new venture into the things of God. As we studied week after week, some of my new friends grew spiritually by leaps and bounds; others seemed not to gain the joy of such an experience. I noticed that whenever someone grasped the importance of setting aside specific time alone with God and with His holy Word, growth always resulted.

Sometimes a student would comment, "I don't seem to love God more each day. Why?"

"How much time do you spend with Him when you are alone?"

"Well, none really. We study here. Isn't that enough?"

"No, not really! This is only one encouragement to lead you into a personal experience with Him for yourself."

To share this was but to share my own innermost needs and the way I had found to satisfy them. In order for me to enjoy the abundant life He offers and to recognize His lovely presence beside me through illness as well as in good health, I needed to spend extra time with Him personally.

My study of the Scriptures with other people helped keep me seeking, yet even this did not suffice for the time alone God and I must have together as close friends. Occasionally, the day began too soon—the phone rang or the doorbell—and away I went, off to the busy world of helping people know God. And suddenly I'd realize that I had rushed off without asking Him to join me.

Finding a quiet, undisturbed time to spend a full hour in prayer and study became a necessity in my schedule, and from those times came the strength of Heaven to pass on to others.*

---

*See the appendix for some of the author's favorite devotional passages.

To keep this hour became very much a battle at times, and the adversary would have it thus. How many times I failed to meet our appointment! Yet how lovingly He waited for me to learn that it was a great loss to me when I missed meeting Him.

I once heard a minister counsel a group of fellow pastors to roll out of bed each morning, not to their feet, but onto their knees—and there dedicate the day to His direction. Then, after the necessary dressing preliminaries, spend a longer period of study and prayer. The simplicity of his method impressed me. Rolling out onto my knees first would certainly place me in the position to ask God to take full charge of all my plans for the day.

Another beautiful way to begin the day with Him, I found, was to say, "Good morning, Lord" when my eyes first opened. There—still in bed—I would ask Him to take over my plans, and I would thank Him for His wonderful love and for the privilege of serving Him.

In addition to this regular schedule for studies, I also returned to my work as a volunteer at the hospital. I was not totally free of pain at all times, yet the regular blood tests looked good and the white count stayed at a normal level. Visiting patients took on new meaning for me. I freely testified of my gratitude that God had spared my life thus far. I hoped that my own experience could lift someone else from discouragement.

My thoughts turned to Beth, a friend who had recently learned that she had leukemia. When I had phoned her after learning of her bad news, she had said, "Oh, I need you to come and tell me about God and the Bible. I don't know much about it, but would like to know, while I'm still here." For a year Beth and I drew closer as friends and closer to Him as we chatted about Him and read some from His Word. Many times she was too ill to concentrate, and at those times prayer seemed especially meaningful to her. Her 5-year-old son stood bravely by, wondering about his mom. Sharp as a little tack, he quickly grasped explanations geared to help him face his motherless future.

Her husband, John—restless, frightened, hopeful each time Beth rallied a bit and devastated the day she took her last breath—tried hard to hang on, hoping our prayers would keep her alive. I had spent hours beside her bed, relieving John when possible. On her last day she told an attendant, "I will go today." As I entered the room I saw her reach up to John. He gently lifted her into his arms in a loving embrace. Shortly afterward, with John close beside her, she breathed her last. Never again would she feel the pain of a dreadful disease.

At that time I had not known the seriousness of my own condition. Now, as I look back, it seems as though it had been a preparation for my own future needs. I desired now all the more to reach out to others to share the One who promised to walk beside us through every difficult situation. It was almost unbearable for me to realize that many faced the same hopeless disease, as well as other types of terminal illness, with no hope. They had no assurance of a better life yet to come.

Years before, working as head housekeeper at the hospital, I had slipped into the room of a dying old man. As I wiped the furniture, I hummed a favorite tune. The patient, swearing, gasping for life, hissed, "What makes you so happy?" I told him that I had a secret which I would share with him. It was my utter belief in God's love, knowing that I could trust Him because of His promises, which had never yet failed and that buoyed up my spirits. His weary head sank back into the pillow, and he sighed, "I wish I could believe—but I can't! I'm an agnostic!"

"But you still could try it His way by just asking Him to come into your life . . ."

"No, no," came his answer. "It's too late for me! I have no hope!" Christian nurses also tried to bring hope into his last few hours—but to no apparent avail. Another Christless grave? Yet our Lord had died to save this child of His.

"Lord, use me wherever You want me to speak a word for You—whether with the ill or with the well. May Your everlasting and powerful love shine through enough to attract others so they can get to know You for what You really are—a God of love." This became, even more than before, my constant prayer, and the answer sometimes led me into unexpected paths.

Many individuals who knew about my serious battle with cancer also observed that I apparently felt quite well, and they wanted to know what had helped me. This gave me many opportunities to speak of the natural remedies that had become a way of life for me. Some chose to try a similar program. They enjoyed the challenges of new food preparations and hoped to keep their bodies in optimum condition. Others left for the twenty-six-day stay at Weimar, reaching out for some definite guidelines so they, too, might enjoy the luxury of the simple life.

Daily there were those to visit in the hospital. It almost seemed as though God had led me into the specialized area of working with cancer patients, and at this point in my own experience this was good. Other cancer victims could relate to my testimony. I tried not to encourage false hope, for some were terminally ill, but I could speak in terms of our preparation for a world to come where sickness and death will never mar existence. I could also explain that God walks beside us even in pain and that He will not allow us to be tempted above that we are able to bear. These thoughts brought courage even to the very ill. Prayer was important to some; others wanted none of it—but I could pray for these people privately and not aggravate them. God dearly loved them too.

My heart sang through these months of activity. "How good You have been to me, my heavenly Father! Could it be, Lord, that I *am* being healed, even though they say there is no cure for myeloma?" The song inside me struck a higher note at the exhilarating thought of such a possibility. Wouldn't that be a tremendous testimony to share with the world?

The more the thought whirled in my head, the more momentum it gained. For a second time I requested special prayer and anointing, and this privilege was given. It wasn't that the first time hadn't been effectual—but didn't even Paul ask three times before God reminded him that His grace would be sufficient? I'm so glad for a heavenly Father who accepts me as I am—weak, faltering, faithless—and allows me to ask many times, even though His own plan for me is and has always been the same. His understanding love draws me ever closer to Him as a magnet draws a piece of metal. Again, at the anointing, I saw no flash of light. All the way home I tried hard to *know* that I was free of all illness, and I spent several quiet hours in prayer and soul searching. I desperately wanted to be sure that I was believing, really believing!

Springtime brightened the days. Hospital visits and Bible studies continued as well as my exercise, diet, and water therapy. Cecil faced many heavy responsibilities as he helped develop plans for a new hospital. To him this was a challenge. And to be involved in a building program, despite its problems and demands, excited him.

Daily we thanked God for the blessings of life, brushing aside thoughts of any possible recurrence of my problems. After all, to believe is to have faith, and to have faith we must not dwell on the negative. And I'm sure that God in heaven took note of our efforts in faith as He continued to lead us just a step at a time into a deeper understanding of what He meant by the word *faith*.

New personnel joined the hospital staff as the time to move into the new hospital approached. Among these came Mary, who took over duties in health education and chaplaincy. Her husband, Paul, became environmental director. As we saw the new facility taking shape, we knew that a little later more doctors would join the staff as well as additional technicians in the various fields of health care.

Mary's role as chaplain naturally brought us into contact almost immediately. Again, God's leading was apparent as we worked together, blending into a close-knit team. I had not been trained as a chaplain; Mary had years of counseling service. I felt that God had led me not only to reach out to others in sharing but also to gain experience and sensitivity from Mary. She, in turn, expressed her joy in having my assistance, as she shouldered her heavy dual role.

The experience of feeling needed brought even more

impetus into my desire to be on the job whenever I could, though I remembered that my first and foremost commitment was to giving Bible studies. It was not always easy to work out an adequate schedule, for husband and home also meant much to me, and duties there had a way of occupying much of my time.

One of my favorite spirituals expressed the feelings that churned within me, and every now and then the words would burst from my lips, "Ain't got time to die!" The song moved with a happy rhythm. It left me thankful all over again for the joy that comes in sharing—not only the sharing in spiritual matters, some would not be interested, but also in befriending those who are friendless or chronically ill. Never did I find any who turned away from a little personal interest in their needs. Sometimes I felt that the benefit that they received as a result of the little I gave was nothing compared to the utter joy and happiness that I gained! This too, I found, was promised in His Holy Writ ages ago. Our Lord wants us to find happiness and health through service to others.

Walking along each day under the predawn stars on my four-mile trek gave opportunity to look up into the star-studded sky and talk to my Friend, who daily revealed to me new avenues for finding peace and gratitude. I could almost seem to hear Him answer, "Yes, My child, 'this is the way, walk ye in it.'"

Thinking of this communication with God reminds me of a busy day at the lunch counter of our former business. There, too, we had hoped that our attitudes and our food service would produce the kind of atmosphere that would reflect God's love to each patron. The dropped ceiling over the main dining area housed soft lighting. The atmosphere was cozy. Jovial, hungry patrons chatted as they enjoyed their meals.

The waitress and I were busy serving from the food-service area. My husband was quietly working on our water heater, which sat high on a platform over the ceiling of the tiny corner restroom. From the serving deck I could glance up and see him at his work. The patrons under the dropped ceiling area could not see him and were not aware of his presence. From time to time I would look up and speak to him. He answered with a word or two and continued at his task.

A gray-bearded, hippy-type man with long, strawlike hair cascading to his shoulders sat perched on a stool nearby. He was intently devouring his sandwich and a bowl of chili beans. He had patronized our lunch counter for some time and from his attitude and conversation I had concluded that he was one who preferred "no religion stuff." This particular day the bearded man suddenly sat up straight, eyes wide in bewilderment as he heard a voice speak from overhead. I had just tossed a quiet question up to my husband, and his answer met the ears of our patron. "What's wrong?" I questioned the man, seeing his look of consternation.

"Oh!" he sighed in relief as he realized a repairman was at work overhead, "I've heard of people talking to Him, but I'd never heard Him answer before!"

I thanked the Lord for His unique ways of reminding people of His existence and supreme power. He really is up there, and we really can hear Him—if not audibly, in His Holy Word as He speaks through it.

Working with Mary an hour or two each day took on a routine that was most rewarding as one by one the assigned patients began to respond to our visits. Now, however, much more than just a visit was involved, because through the chaplain's gentle guidance I was learning how to help families make proper arrangements for financial affairs when a loved one was in a terminal condition. The response to my carefully framed questions was usually overwhelming gratitude that they could open up and talk about the things they had feared to discuss and yet knew must be broached. It was then possible to encourage them to reach out to their own attorneys or other counselors for any legal aid they might need. Once these needs were met, the family and the patient felt more at ease and comfortable.

Learning other areas of need and how to meet them was all part of serving the patients. I relished being able to provide more than just friendly patient calls.

My heart sang vibrantly every now and then when, on opening a patient's door, I would meet the eyes of one I had known as a customer or someone from one of the churches in the community where it had often been my privilege to bring a message in song. Already friends, we would chat about the particular needs of the moment that this person might have as a patient in our hospital.

As I slipped into a room early one morning, my new patient's broad smile told me she already knew me. We soon discovered our common ground and immediately began building what has become an enduring friendship. Juanita, a blonde and very attractive lady, suffered severe problems involving cancer. The surgeons had succeeded in removing the tumor, but complications with her heart brought anxious moments for her husband and those of us standing by.

Juanita loved the Lord in her own way. Though she did not attend church regularly, she was always eager for our prayer time. Since both of us battled cancer, our prayers and talks together produced a bond that could not have been formed otherwise. Soon she was up and around, and then the happy day came when she returned home. Much later God's love was reciprocated back to me through this lovely friend.

Fred, another patient dying of cancer, thrilled with every prayer, every mention of our Father's love. He shared with me gems of thought and Scripture that had fed his soul through many years of fighting the disease. He showed a markedly different outlook as he approached death in comparison with another patient down the hall who suffered from almost identical physical problems. I thanked God for Fred's testimony, realizing that he lifted my spirits probably more than my visits encouraged him.

It wasn't many months later that, as I glanced through the local paper, Fred's smiling face again bespoke his total trust. The article below his picture accentuated the serenity of his facial expression. I read on and thrilled at his personal testimony. He spoke to the whole community about God's goodness all through his years of severe pain. He mentioned his appreciation for the fine medical attention he had received within the local hospital. And there before my eyes I saw my own name! What was he saying? My heart melted at his specific expression of appreciation for the visits Mary and I had made to his hospital bedside.

Fred closed his eyes quietly a short time later, still showing that beautiful, totally peaceful trust. No longer does he endure the gnawing pain of disease, and soon he will awake with life eternal. Then the Saviour will forever be his constant, visible companion, and there will be "no more death, neither sorrow, nor crying, neither shall there be any more pain" (Rev. 21:4).

The "quiet room," adjacent to the chaplain's office, offered a secluded place of comfort for families waiting through a surgery, taking turns visiting a very ill family member, or finding temporary respite from grief over the loss of a loved one. We in the chaplain's office became keenly aware that visitors to this room welcomed a few words of encouragement or just our presence. Tears often flowed freely, but this was good; they provided release. "Tears are a language that God understands" one song declares, and through the tears came opportunities for us to share love and concern.

There was the man of American-Indian descent. Since his cancer was very similar to my own, we spent some time comparing our experiences. He took me on a long, imaginary journey through his past life, and it was evident that he had "come up by his own bootstraps." He had reared a family and built a comfortable home, surrounded by hundreds of roses that he had nurtured personally. He was an artist and a craftsman of great skill. He wanted me to see his home, so I made an appointment with his wife to show me through their place. It overflowed with the results of his artistry, and the yard looked like a floral nursery. Such care, such time, such love must have gone into the making of this home! Added to his talents were those of his wife in needlecraft and art.

Yet now, as he faced his future, Alec was devastated. Life did not seem worth continuing. He wanted to die, and did not want to think about arranging for the welfare of those left behind. The horror of his plight had taken a terrible toll upon his rational thinking. We had many frank talks as I shared with him the peace that comes from having our affairs in order. And, finally, one day he agreed, for the sake of his wife and for his own peace of mind, to seek proper aid in caring for his business affairs. Quickly his spirits picked up, and it was a joy to walk into his room and see a smile on his face.

Some, as it was with Alec, we never see again after their hospital stay. Yet I thank God for him, for the life story he shared, and for the opportunity to receive the blessings that come when we cast our bread upon the waters (see Eccl. 11:1).

As a result of my own experiences with one patient after another, my own apprehension of what the future might bring seemed less and less to burden me. There was much too much to live for. Even in adversity and with less than complete health, I could still be of service. It was exciting, rewarding! It brought "health to my bones" and a song to my lips, and I thanked God for the privilege.

Where was my Father leading? What lessons in faith did He still desire for me to learn? Would He use me even more in the future as I submitted to His guidance? He had used Fred. He had used Juanita. How was He going to use me? Fred's testimony had come to a beautiful close. Now he could rest—but his works would surely follow him. Would my life continue to improve, as it seemed to be doing? What lay ahead?

Picking Up the Pieces

The questions in my mind concerning God's particular plan for my existence loomed large at times. However, my busy life as I continued to teach, to assist the chaplain, and to maintain other routine schedules soon dispelled these heavy thoughts. It was enough just to be here and to spend time with others.

July rolled around again, and once more we had the opportunity for ten days of rest and spiritual uplift at our favorite spot. The familiar grounds of our yearly camping retreat beckoned invitingly. Two years before had been so different—so painful. This year held promise of my being able to enjoy these few days in more comfort.

Together a friend and I hiked up the mountainous road, around the bends, and down the slopes. We drank in the beauty and breathed deeply of the fir-scented aromas. Far below us the winding river twisted like a piece of blue ribbon.

Walking on, I felt a twinge of pain flare for a moment in my pelvis. It disappeared almost before I could recognize it as anything unusual. For some time I had not taken any pain medication, having no need of it. The resulting clearness of mind had been such a pleasure compared to the sleepiness I fought when its use had been necessary. I recalled the terrible pain I had suffered two years before, when I had not had any medication with me. What a relief to have that twinge go away so fast! But, no, a little farther down the road, and there it was again—more pronounced this time.

"It must be just a hitch in my get-along," I pondered, so I

said nothing to anyone about it. It couldn't be a recurrence of active cancer cells in the bone—not after nearly two years! Not after my careful health-sustaining program.

God knew that during this time of remission I had become quite active for Him again. He had heard the many prayers in my behalf from all across the country and from nearly every church in our community. He had heard the special prayers at the anointing service.

I was sure God must only be testing my faith, and I would prove that my faith had grown. Dismissing the thought of the pain from my mind seemed the best way to demonstrate my growth.

During the rest of the encampment a few flare-ups of pain bothered me, but generally I felt comfortable enough to have a pleasant stay and to enjoy the music and lectures. All too soon the time came to return home. Now I knew that I must squarely face this new aggravation. I checked in with our family doctor, who scheduled more X-rays. It was a real support to know these doctors and technicians as friends. At first no evidence surfaced on the X-ray, which puzzled the doctors. We could all feel the bump, indicating another tumor, yet the picture was not clear because of the location of the culprit. The doctor recommended further radiation. Recognizing that, with another tumor evident, this was no doubt the best course to pursue, I agreed and made preparation for radiation treatments once again. At first, with business arrangements that I needed to expedite and having overcome my early fears of the treatment, all went smoothly and routinely. Then, one evening, like the onrush of a great tidal wave crashing over me, I was swept ruthlessly out into an ocean of dreaded fears.

What had happened?

Didn't I trust God enough?

Didn't He want me to show the world that living close to Him and in harmony with His natural laws would restore health?

Didn't He need me to encourage those who were giving up? Didn't He need me to tell them of His love for them—even in their adversities?

Wasn't He making me well so others, too, could hope for the good results that come from totally trusting Him?

My tears flowed more freely now, soaking my pillow at night, dampening my husband's shoulder in unexpected outbursts, and drenching tissues when I daydreamed of future years with my precious grandchildren.

The questions persisted: How do I relate to other cancer patients now? What hope can I extend to them? God, where are You leading in this experience? You aren't handling it the way I thought You were! How can I be strengthened through this experience? How can anyone else be strengthened by it?

I had heard that people who face grief, loss, or terminal illness often go through certain phases, and I began to recognize my own association with them through my mood changes. After I had endured a good cry, most often the whole world took on a brighter look, and I was able to search for answers to my many questions. The phases included:

Denial—not accepting the truth of the existing problem.

Bargaining—"Lord, if You'll heal, I'll do so much for You!"

Withdrawal—not talking about the problem and withdrawing within oneself.

Anger—"Why me? It's not fair!"

Acceptance—finally, accepting the situation.

Had I been bargaining with God in thinking that He owed me life in exchange for my telling people about Him?

I returned to His Word, and He reminded me of things He had pointed out before. He had not made promises that fit my earthly, finite plans. He had already shown me that in this world I would have troubles. Something kept saying, "Deeper, My child. Dig deeper into My Word. Spend more time with Me and you will understand more of how My love for you includes much more than you can visualize or plan. Dig deeper and learn to trust Me through whatever comes." I thought I had learned that trust, and now I felt as if I were back at the beginning of the track!

Recalling Job's story, I turned to the book bearing his name and reviewed his experience. Why did God take away all Job's children and then strike him with all those sores? What a picture we imagine at times! As I read again the first chapters of the story, I began to recognize who had brought the disaster to Job.

According to the first few verses of chapter one, Job was plainly a man of God. God called him perfect, a good man, His own follower. The report goes on to explain that the sons of God came to present themselves before the Lord—and Satan came also. God asked him to explain his presence, and he replied that he came from "going to and fro in the earth."

God asked him another question: "Have you noticed My good man Job down there? A perfect and upright man."

"Yes," Satan responded, "but You've put a hedge around him. No wonder he serves You! Lift that hedge and see if he doesn't curse You to Your face!"

Then the Lord gave Satan permission to try Job, and Satan—not God—set out to destroy all Job's children. But in spite of the agony of his tremendous loss, Job continued to praise God and trust Him totally through it all. Even Job didn't understand the circumstances of Satan's bargaining and cried out, "The Lord gave, and the Lord hath taken away. Blessed be the name of the Lord!" (chap. 1:21). But an adversary had done the "taking away," endeavoring to put the blame on God.

But Satan wasn't satisfied. Again he challenged God, saying, "Put forth thine hand now, and touch his bone and his flesh, and he will curse thee to thy face." The Lord did not put forth His hand to touch him, but He did accept Satan's challenge: "He is in thine hand; but save his life." Then Satan "went forth from the presence of the Lord, and smote Job with sore boils from the sole of his foot unto his crown." Again Satan, as always, did the dirty work. Satan is the *destroyer*. God is the *restorer* in every battle between good and evil.

Challenging God! Accusing God of playing favorites with His special people who do everything His way! Isn't that just like the devil?

I wondered how God could have handled this challenge any other way. He knew Job and He trusted him enough to allow the scenario to be played out. Satan also needed to know the kind of person Job was. And the world needed to know it, and at that point I needed to know it.

It dawned on me that Job had proved to the universe that with a vital and constant connection with God a human being can remain faithful through any adversity. Job—a mere man—has gone down in the history of the universe as an example of one afflicted by the devil, the mighty being who himself had to be expelled from God's heavenly courts and who was still very angry over his loss.

It seemed to me that my own experience somewhat paralleled Job's. I had not lost ten children, but one in my family had been severely afflicted and the hurt of that experience was still with me. Could Satan have possibly challenged God concerning me? Now it was "skin for skin," or, in my case, bone for bone. Had God permitted Satan access to me, to my body, to let Satan know that I, too, would remain faithfully His own? I wasn't Job—no great, well-known patriarch from Biblical history. Why me? Just a speck of humanity down here in modern times. Yet Peter had warned in New Testament times: "Be sober, be vigilant; because your adversary the devil, as a roaring lion, walketh about, seeking whom he may devour" (1 Peter 5:8).

And Paul said that "all these things happened unto them for ensamples: and they are written for our admonition, upon whom the ends of the world are come" (1 Cor. 10:11). So Satan must definitely still be up to his old tricks, trying to prove God a tyrant clear down through the ages until "the ends of the world are come."

Yes, he would use me; Satan would use anyone he could reach. He had used many others throughout the ages and would continue until his great conflict with God would be forever ended, and the universe would be able to plainly recognize the real culprit: not God, but this sneaky destroyer, this liar (John 8:44), this deceiver (Rev. 12:9), the devil himself. Yet it would take proof—tangible examples of how he has dealt with human beings in contrast with the dealings of a loving God.

Could it be that God was allowing me to experience this trauma as a result of another of Satan's challenges?

I could almost hear the archdeceiver saying, "There's another one, God, that You've hedged around, protected. Of course she's Your subject! Why shouldn't she be? All her life she's had it good. No special upsets in her life. She has enjoyed a large, happy, loving family. She's been healthy. She loves life. She loves people. She loves You, God, and gives You all the credit. But just try lifting Your protective hedge, try touching her with affliction, try hurting her family, and You'll see how long she'll last on Your side!"

And I could hear my loving God, as He ignored Satan's suggestion to touch me with affliction, say: "If you must, Satan, go ahead and put her through your tests. She is Mine, and she will remain so because she trusts Me totally for her strength."

As I saw the similarities, suddenly a thrill went through my being. As it was of old with Job, so it could be with me in the twentieth century. I determined that, like Job, I would trust Him totally. What an honor to become personally involved in this tremendous controversy, knowing, from the Bible, that God's side will ultimately win.

Again I remembered that Jesus had said, "In the world ye shall have tribulation" (John 16:33), but He also said, "I will never leave thee, nor forsake thee" (Heb. 13:5).

But what about the New Testament and Jesus Christ? Did He ever make it clear who brings pain and hurt and death? As I leafed through the pages of Dr. Luke's Gospel I found the story of the woman bent over with an infirmity for eighteen long years (chap. 13:10-17). Jesus had been teaching in the local synagogue on the Sabbath day when He noticed this poor, bent-over woman. In His loving manner He spoke to her, reached out and touched her, simply saying, "Woman, thou art loosed from thine infirmity." Suddenly, she could stand straight and tall again, and she praised God for her healing. It all caused quite a stir. The church leaders were shocked at such Sabbathbreaking and reproved Jesus angrily for His action. Jesus, in response, reminded them that they themselves would untie an ox from his stall and lead him to water on the Sabbath, and yet—and here was His clincher—"ought not this woman . . . whom Satan hath bound, lo, these eighteen years, be loosed from this bond on the sabbath day?"

God had not bound her; Satan had. Here, Jesus Christ, the One who spoke the worlds into existence (Heb. 1:1, 2), plainly exposed the source and the instigator of all pain. And here again He took Satan's devastating actions and brought a beautiful blessing out of it.

Satan, the destroyer—God, the restorer!

These accounts began to settle many of the questions that had tormented me as the reality of my condition became more apparent. The questions were not all answered, nor did I expect that they might ever be, yet a deepening experience of trust grew stronger within me.

No, I could not measure God's love for me by the extent of disasters in my life. Because I lived in this world where sin abounds, disasters could come my way. The "prince of this world" (John 12:31) would do all in his power to see to that.

Yet, as the old song says, "This world is not my home." My chief concern is to look for "a city which hath foundations, whose builder and maker is God" (Heb. 11:10). Through this perspective, even the day-by-day battles here on earth have become a challenge in my own life, making it a joy to be involved; making it exciting to live; making time now become quality time—not just a passing of time from sunup to sunset as at first it seemed it would be while living with a terminal disease. Could God still use me to help others who suffer? Yes! Now it would be more possible than before. No longer could anyone say, "You don't understand. You've never been there!"

Yes, God, You certainly didn't handle this as I had thought, or as I had planned. "Neither are your ways my ways" (Isa. 55:8). You've had to remind me often, but thank You for this—Your better way. Teach me now to praise Your name more and more as learning to trust You continues to become even a higher experience within my life.

"God is our refuge and strength, a very present help in

trouble. Therefore will not we fear, though the earth be removed, and though the mountains be carried into the midst of the sea; though the waters thereof roar and be troubled, though the mountains shake with the swelling thereof" (Ps. 46:1-3).

I would have had You take away the pain, but You saw my need for trust. I would that You had left with me my life of ease, yet You looked ahead and allowed disease. You have suffered, too, as You took my hand and walked so close that inch by inch Your strength became my strength, and You became my ever-present Guide.

The blow had been a heavy one. However, as I landed in the pits of despair after such a build-up of hopes based upon my own set of values, my own understanding of how God's mighty power would be clarified. Crawling out from under the murky miasma of my own concept into the shining solidarity of His perfect plan, I felt better prepared for the future. I wondered—ever so cautiously—how the months ahead would deal with me. Even yet, trust had room for growth, but my heavenly Father knew and would allow only as much as I could bear. He would allow no more than that. This He had promised.

I read accounts in the Scriptures of God's refining His people through affliction (see Isa. 48:10). "I will . . . refine them as silver is refined, and will try them as gold is tried: they shall call on my name, and I will hear them: I will say, It is my people: and they shall say, The Lord is my God" (Zech. 13:9). So this is how He takes the evil of the destroyer and brings good through it!

Could I share this truth with those who thus far could not see it? Could I myself have believed it before experiencing it? No, I had not seen this fulness of His love that dipped so deeply into experimental growth right where it hurts.

Little did I know how much more room for growth there was. Nor could I see the road ahead to realize the walk that still lay before me.

Soon after the radiation series, my pain let up, so we drove to Yosemite for a Christmas family reunion. Traveling in our van made the trip very comfortable, and although I felt a little weak, I was thrilled to be with Mom and all the brothers and sisters, as well as with Cecil's mom and brother and wife. We thoroughly "lived up" the few days together in the beauty of our surroundings.

By April I needed additional radiation therapy. Friends came to my rescue again by taking turns transporting me to my appointments. This time it seemed a bit less traumatic.

The forthcoming visit of our daughter Pat and her children, Ricky and Cindy, filled all our thoughts, and on May 28 they arrived. What an exciting day! Who wouldn't feel better? Pat drove me to my appointments for radiation. These were the crowning days for Pat and me as we spent much time together, dreading that it would end in a couple of weeks.

After Cecil and I took Pat and the children to the airport, we took our time driving around San Francisco, seeing the sights, taking a boat cruise out through the Golden Gate, and stopping for lunch. We wanted to be together in our loneliness after having said goodbye to Pat and the children. None of this was planned. These seemed like soothing strokes of earthly recompense that God was giving in return for what He was asking of me.

In a few days we would celebrate forty years of marriage. We decided to take time off and spend three weeks on a trip. Could I handle it? With the van, yes! Let's go!

South of the Border

On June 29, our fortieth anniversary, we nosed our little van onto the highway and headed south. Both Cecil and I looked forward to a pleasurable three weeks of vacation. During this time I would also continue my search for health, but we said little about this to our friends lest they get the idea we were going off on some tangent.

I had recently counseled with a doctor friend who had explained the values of a serum for body immune buildup, and this keenly interested me. We would take our vacation and look into the serum treatment at the same time. Our doctor friend and his wife had graciously invited us to their area, and so we had decided to travel south.

Our family doctor knew about our trip, as did a few other friends and relatives. With the comfortable bed in the van, I made the trip in comparative comfort—the wear and tear being more on Cec, who had to do all the driving.

Toward evening the day we left, we stopped to eat out, celebrating our anniversary, and upon returning to the van we sat looking quizzically at a pretty package handed us by our friends before we left home. They said we must wait to open it until this moment—and the time had come!

Carefully unfolding the pretty wrap, we hurried into the package and found $100 in $20 bills. A lump stuck in my throat as I realized the sacrifice these good friends had made in order to help us buy gas for our trip. We shook our heads gratefully, thanked our Father for such a blessing, then headed south on the highway, driving into the night.

I dropped off to sleep while Cec chose to drive during the cool of the night. Some time later I stirred from sound sleep to realize that Cec had pulled into a rest stop. Soon he had stretched out comfortably on the padded floor of the van for some well-earned sleep himself.

We arrived at our destination near the Mexican border around noon the next day. Margaret, the wife of our doctor friend, was hospitably preparing a meal for us. She had grown up in our hometown with our two girls, so she was like one of our own family. Seeing her again bridged the many years since those days of her early childhood. Chatting away, we emerged from yesteryear into Margaret's modern-day world with her lovely Spanish-style home, swimming pool, and hot tub.

Later Tom, her husband, arrived home. He invited us to spend our three-week stay in their guest house half a block away. Simon, Tom's young cousin, had recently joined their household, and he busily kept the garden in shape, singing lustily as he worked. We came to love Simon dearly.

We found that a chiropractic doctor, also a business promoter and Tom's right-hand counselor in an area of his business world, occupied our room on a part time basis. They called him "Dr. T," since his Iranian name was too difficult to repeat often. Two other people temporarily were living in the quarters, but they would move before long. So this was our temporary home and one that we enjoyed very much throughout our stay.

My immune-therapy shots would begin the next day at Dr. Tom's office across the border in Tijuana. On that day we also met a couple of lovely ladies from Canada, one of whom was an arthritic patient, who also would take the series of shots. They dressed immaculately and drove a fancy Cadillac. They had spent eight months south of the border and had tried many other methods before they heard of Dr. Tom's care. Within a week the patient's health had improved so much that they decided to return home.

Dr. Tom took us on a lovely tour of the area. We visited some places known for health "cures" and saw the modern section versus the old section of town—from the very poor to the very rich, the sublime to the ridiculous.

Each day we ground through customs to get to and from Tijuana, because I needed to check in with Dr. Tom regularly. His was a careful, honest practice of medicine. He had dedicated himself to aiding those patients who needed help for their many maladies. Across the border the practice of medicine took on various forms, depending upon the type of problems to be dealt with.

As in any other area, so in Mexico; there are honest and dishonest people with whom to deal. We learned that in traveling to Mexico for cancer therapy, one needs to be acquainted with one's own illness. What are the available local treatment programs, and one's own prospects? What form of illness does one have, and where will the treatment be given? Unfortunately, it seems that politics and greed often influence the business of health treatment in other countries, just as it does in the U.S. We were most grateful to know a reputable medical doctor whom we could trust.

The doctor soon helped me establish a regular schedule. Drinks of herb teas and juices, careful diet, IVs, vitamin C in large dosages, all became a part of my program.

One happy day, despite much pain on my part, Dr. T, Dr. Tom and Margaret, Cec and I drove the van far down the coast. We wanted to explore the country a bit and enjoy the beautiful coastline. We visited a deserted resort area that had seen more active times and marveled at the beauty of the place. Its stone steps stretched all the way to the beautiful beach far below.

The bed in the van afforded me its usual comfort, making the trip pleasant in spite of the discomfort in my neck. On some days we drove around to see the sights of San Diego. On other days we parked at the beach and watched the surfers at play. While my condition hampered our activities, we still enjoyed the days of relaxation together.

The three weeks passed quickly, and we soon had to bid farewell to Margaret and Tom, their two children, Simon, and Dr. T. How much value I received from the immune shots is difficult to ascertain. I do feel that it helped me make a comeback following surgery a couple of months later. The bounce back seems to have been, as we believe, miraculous. Perhaps God has used some natural remedy such as this to give me more precious time. I do know that those three weeks of chatting, caring, and praying together drew Cecil and me closer together than ever before.

Thank God for the closeness of our forty years together. This one ended the best of all!

Growing Together Through Sharing

As brothers and sisters grow up together they learn that adjustments must be made in order to live together. In marriage, the learning begins at a stage when each partner has already decided the specific way he or she wants to deal with a tube of toothpaste (squeeze it in the middle or roll it systematically). Each has developed definite preferences in foods and in how they are prepared. The blending processes of two lives at this stage sometimes take on a bit more trauma than the developments earlier in life.

Starry-eyed on our wedding day, I knew that whatever adjustments would come for my handsome young husband and I—they would be a breeze. After all, we had spent hours discussing the reasons why so many marriages fail. We felt sure that these reasons were not part of our lives.

We both liked and disliked many of the same things. Our religious affiliations were the same. We each grew up in a family with several children. True, we chose to marry before finishing college, and we recognized that we would need to continue our studies under more difficult circumstances than when we were single. But our love ran deep and true, and we knew we could hurdle any obstacle.

Our first tiny home, within walking distance of the college, had been built by my dad. It was exciting to unpack our beautiful wedding gifts, admire them again, and set them in their proper places. What fun, having a home of our own!

As I began frying an egg the next morning, I asked my sweet groom how he liked his eggs fixed. I then set about to fry them just the way he described. He didn't register the delight I expected and finally said, "It's pretty good, but Mom used to . . ." For a moment I saw red, then I decided to let him show me how "Mom used to . . ." Later I learned from Mom that she had seldom prepared eggs to his satisfaction either, so I ceased being too concerned and found by then that he had come to enjoy my cooking.

I took extreme offense at hearing him describe my gravy as "poverty paste," until I learned that his family had raised dairy cows and so had enjoyed an abundance of pure cream for making gravy. Anything made without cream was termed "poverty paste" at their house.

We'd been on our own—away from both families—for about a week when I found my young groom sitting quietly and looking a bit lonely. "What's the matter?" I asked.

"I don't know! I guess I miss my brothers!"

The adjustments had begun, and even *we* would have our share to make. Now we look back and enjoy a good chuckle as we recollect those first few months of marriage.

We would come to realize that the learning processes continue throughout life. Even when we thought we had learned them all, a whole new package opened before us. We would learn to protect each other from hurts and then have to learn how to allow each other to face the hurts and share them, resolving them as a unit.

And so in the early stages of my battle with cancer, I found it difficult to let Cec know the extent of my pain. Each time he did sense it, I saw the stark horror that flashed across his face. Couldn't I save him from this? Perhaps it was enough that I should feel it. Little did I realize that in his close contact with the medical profession in his work, he knew more about my condition than I did and was protecting me from the information he had.

During the first weeks and months of my illness, I reserved my tears for the privacy of my own pillow after he was fast asleep. And this helped carry me through the days and evenings together. God knew my tears. He also knew Cec's, but we kept our feelings hidden from each other.

The night came when I was very ill. My physician told me that I must check into the hospital. The same night news came of Dad's death. I looked at Cec as I hung up the telephone then crumpled on the couch, and the tears came. "Cec, I can't handle this! I'm so sick—and now Dad's gone!" As I cried on his strong shoulder, it became clear that I needed his support more than I had admitted, and I thanked God for him—and for the relief that came from letting go.

Soon I felt more comfortable with this openness, and, with my freedom, it seemed that Cec, too, could share more frankly with me. There was the time when, only semiconscious, I quoted Scripture aloud; and he bent near to encourage me and to pray aloud for me. God had blessed me with a faithful husband! Even later, as my life hung in the balance, we found ourselves able to talk openly about death and the will and our children. I know that this could never have happened except for the step-by-step process of learning together. By sharing our deeper feelings, we enjoyed a closeness that we had never experienced heretofore.

Much later, we found it possible, even necessary, to talk through very difficult matters, even areas that seemed best to avoid discussing until I had regained my strength. But I could find no inner rest unless I knew that any problem—bad news, financial difficulties, or whatever—could be discussed and resolved together. We both concluded that this was the only way for us to live with whatever would come in the future.

So it was that through friends, through my own blood relatives, and through my husband came great support and encouragement. Through my in-laws came a whole set of special blessings. Cec's four brothers, their wives, their families, and their mother were ready at all times to bolster our courage. No wonder my own countenance could register joy!

The Value of Family

"Mother, can I have a Gramma Steen apple?" My younger daughter was 5 at the time.

"A what, Beth?"

"A Gramma Steen apple!" I wondered how she tied her favorite kindergarten teacher in with a desire for an apple. Grandma Steen was a monument of love. Her tiny students sang her songs all week—but apples? What did she mean? Then it dawned! We had purchased a box of Gravenstein apples. She had heard us call them by name, but the word had sounded to her like the name of her teacher.

Bouncing little Beth with the long, brown pigtails! Always and forever thinking things through in her own inimitable fashion! And her curiosity and courage seemed boundless. When she was only 2 she managed to climb a ladder to the steep rooftop. Later she tumbled off a ledge and landed on the ground eight feet below. Each time she survived unscathed.

Her ability to attract a crowd of playmates into our yard always amazed me. One evening I glanced out the back door on a total disarray of toys, cans, bottles, and junk strewn generously between our home and the neighbor's. Calling my 5-year-old, I instructed her to clean up the mess. She objected loudly, saying she didn't make all the mess. I left her to her dilemma and hurried off to prepare supper. Suddenly the door flew open, and big sister, Pat, angrily fumed, "Beth's out there with *my* piggy bank, paying all the kids to pick up the toys!"

Pat, four and one-half years older, usually carried her seniority with dignity and patience, though her sister's lack of these virtues periodically left her totally chagrined. With the span of age difference it would continue to seem so to her until both reached young adult years and their personalities became a complement one to the other.

Being a family unit means growth, not only for the children but also for Father and Mother. The beautiful love we experienced was expressed with hugs and kisses, many free times of frolicking together, riding Father's back "horsy-back" style, playing peekaboo.

Pat enjoyed protecting her curly-headed 3-month-old cousin whenever he was sunning in his bassinet. One day she decided on her own initiative to brush those curls briskly with her own stiff hairbrush. On another occasion she shared her grapes with him, shoving one after another into his tiny, rosebud mouth until his mother heard him gagging and ran to the rescue.

I tucked our girls in at night with prayers and a hug during their young years, but when they reached school age, my own expressions of love became a bit more dignified, because I assumed that they might prefer to be more "grown up." One night, when Beth was about 10, she had trotted off to bed, but soon called, "Mother." I hastened to her room. She looked up with a sheepish grin and said, "Tuck me in, Mom." I had been mistaken about feelings of growing up!

Through the busy years that came and went, our loving heavenly Father knew of our needs for growth and helped us improve our ways to express our deep love for one another. Later we developed a successful bakery and store business, where the girls and I could work side by side through their high school and college days. We soon became so busy that times for relaxation became rare. We managed to keep a good sense of humor, and I personally loved the work. Yet it took a heavy toll. One day as Pat looked at my tired face tears welled up in her blue eyes and she said, "Mom, it's too much for you and all of us! I want a mother, and this takes all your time!"

I assured her we must stick with it, for it gave us an opportunity to work together while earning the extra money needed for school. No more was said. Stick with it we did, and the girls worked hard during summers and holidays. Soon they were attending boarding schools at some distance from home. I plunged even deeper into the rush of business, working with faithful employees and seldom having time for a jaunt to visit our girls. When we could get away, we spent the happy hours catching up on their latest interests.

For thirteen years the hurry-scurry of business tended to blur the original picture we had cherished of a relaxed family life style, though we also enjoyed many fun times together when we'd head for the coast in our camper and pickup and spend a weekend together. The girls would pack and load the camper while I continued decorating cakes up to the last moment. One week we'd had enough, so we closed the store, hung up a sign that read "No Bread This Week—We're Loafin'," and headed for the mountains.

Our employees were amiable, cheerful individuals. They worked faithfully and shared a punch line of humor when the schedule tightened to a tense situation. My own mind occasionally played tricks on me, and I'd act hastily when more deliberate planning could have saved time in the long run.

The whole crew and our girls never let die the story of my most striking example in "haste makes waste." In addition to my weekly routine, I spent one hour teaching singing to a private kindergarten-primary school across town. This particular day was unusually busy at the store, and time was pressing in on me. It was graduation day for the tiny tots. We had planned a special program in which my little singers would warble lustily for their parents. Our bakery had, as a special treat, prepared little pies for each child. With no time to spare I had hurriedly dressed and whisked the large tray of pies to the waiting station wagon and in so doing caught a disdainful glance at the layer of dust on the surface of the car.

Slamming the door tightly, I impetuously grabbed the nearby water hose and tried to spray off the film of dust. I dropped the hose, in my haste not noticing that the end of it had hooked over the bumper. Jumping into the car, I turned the key, raced the motor, and zoomed the short distance down the driveway to the street. Quickly I glanced both ways for traffic, stepped on the gas, and turned north. I sensed a strange pull on the car, followed by a release, but I didn't look back. There was no time for delay!

I sped up State Street to Gobbi, turned east and zipped on down across the railroad track past Leslie Street and on to Orchard. Careening around the corner, I could see a line of sleek, shiny cars—the parents had arrived for the performance of their small fry. I skidded into a parking place and jumped from the car. There for fifty feet down the road behind me trailed a long, green garden hose attached to the bumper! But that wasn't all. On the far end of the hose dangled a three-foot piece of pipe and a faucet. Lest anyone should see what I brought with me, I took time to reel in the hose, picturing meanwhile some sort of geyser going on at home—but there wasn't time for that now. The show must go on!

What we sang for the mommies and daddies that day wasn't uppermost in my mind during that endless hour. When I arrived back at homebase, things were wet but I found no geyser. Walking into the store, I asked our clerk, "What happened out here? Everything is wet!" I learned that 85-year-old Grandpa had taken stock of the problem and managed to get the water under control, but he was still out looking for the faucet!

Wedding bells rang one warm August day. Pat and her young groom skipped happily down the long aisle of the church and before long were headed East to begin their life in the ministry. Smiling with joy for them, but weeping at the thought of the distance between us, her father, sister, and I turned back to the busy life at home and the store.

In three years it was time for another wedding and another joyful and then tearful experience when Beth, too, walked down the same aisle. She left the home fires to also become the wife of a minister, and they moved halfway across the United States.

Throwing ourselves into our work, Cec and I began the adjustment every parent experiences once the youngsters have flown from the nest. We waited eagerly for letters, vacation times, and phone calls.

Later we sold our business, and I began teaching the Bible and doing some volunteer work. No longer did we need to endure the pressures that had so long been stressful. It also afforded time now for reflection. Strange that our close-knit family should end up so separated by distance. More than ever before my motherly protectiveness began to surface. I determined that the girls would see only the happy side of our life. They must never worry about us for any reason—and at first this presented no problem, as life moved on at a steady pace, with only minor upsets. We seemed always to hear happiness and glowing reports from them, too.

Grandbabies came, bringing thrills of excitement and joy when we could spend time with them on rare occasions. Five or six years elapsed. Christmas was just around the corner once again. We all planned to celebrate the holiday together for the first time since the girls had left home. What exuberance! How I cooked and planned and decorated! Two weeks more, and they would all join us.

The phone rang one evening, and I heard the strained voice of our son-in-law. He told us that Pat was very ill in the hospital. Our world fell apart. How could it be? Pat was never ill! Why, God? Why? Oh, why?

Eventually they flew out. Beth and Les arrived also, and together we all worked to help our sick girl regain her health. For some months she and her two babies stayed on at our home as she recuperated. Wayne was able to stay by only part of the time, however.

At times she would question, "Why me, Mom? I've never been sick!" And we shared together such promises as "Count it all joy . . ." In *not* understanding we began to experience the deeper values of trust and faith. We read John's greeting to his friend Gaius: "Beloved, I wish above all things that thou mayest prosper and be in health, even as thy soul prospereth" (3 John 2). And David's inspired words encouraged us: "Bless the Lord, O my soul: and all that is within me, bless his holy name. Bless the Lord, O my soul, and forget not all his benefits: who forgiveth all thine iniquities; who healeth all thy diseases" (Ps. 103:1-3). As we read such Scriptures, we were drawn moment by moment into a special relationship with our loving Father in heaven, one that could only have been gained through suffering.

Much later, during my own battle with myeloma, Pat brought her two children, now 8 and 7 years old, to spend over two weeks with us. We camped out in the redwoods and spent three days on the coast. We chatted about rocks and stamp collections with Ricky and Cindy and remembered old times with their mother. I was having a series of radiation treatments as well. Pat and I spent many hours together as she drove me to the hospital for treatment. Never before had I leaned so much upon her for strength, and never before had the bond between us seemed so firm. No longer did I need to protect her. She was a mature woman. Her companionship grew deeper in the pain we had shared together.

And there was Beth. Worn from an eighteen-hundred-mile drive with a 9-month-old baby, Beth had walked into her sister's sickroom and had quickly sized up her sister's needs. Together with her husband, Les, and with Wayne, she had shouldered much of the responsibilities—staying by for over a month to help.

There were other times from year to year when we were able to spend time together, and again—though I had always desired to protect this baby of mine from hurts—it became evident that Beth, too, had grown up and would prefer to share with us rather than be sheltered in times of crisis.

The crisis came for me not long after Pat's visit. My own life hung in the balance for two weeks. The phone rang frequently between California, Connecticut, and Iowa. Should they come? Cec, doing his best to be a strong father, admonished them not to make the trip. He would keep them posted. They assured him that they would come whenever he said the word.

Finally, Beth and Les, who had not seen us for over a year, called the hospital and talked to my husband. They told him that they could stand it no longer; they would drive to California just as soon as they could get things together.

The fact that they took command at that particular moment, overwhelmed Cec. He returned to my room in tears—but, strangely enough, they were tears of relief.

Three days later, three tiny, big-eyed babies and two weary adults descended upon my room. Tears flowed freely and words tumbled out—words of relief, words of gratitude—punctuated with precious moments of silence. The crisis hour banished all formalities, all pretense, all overprotectiveness. We shared and shared alike in the pain and realization of the uncertainties that might lie ahead.

God's guidance wove in and out through the experiences of our family, ever drawing the golden thread of His love around us. He strengthened us with trust and faith and built for us a foundation strong in His strength. We learned to recognize in one another traits that we had often taken for granted.

The thought began to dawn on me that over the years I had taken for granted my own parents and brothers and sisters. No, I had not forgotten my mother, father, and eight brothers and sisters. But I had not always verbalized my affection. Through the years it had become an accepted fact that words were not always necessary to express our innermost feelings. We had grown up together, learning to share and share alike, learning not to be crybabies. But one by one, as each left home, we sensed a certain vacancy that no other could fill.

Not until I became a mother did I realize how long and hard Mom and Dad had worked to keep us fed, clothed, and educated. Surely they must have felt relieved to have one less expense! How wrong I was! After I became ill, Mom spent many hours with me. Always stoic, always cheerful, she never shed a tear in my presence. Then one day following a telephone call concerning a family wedding, I burst into tears. Mom rushed to my side, took my hand, and asked, "What's the matter?"

"I want to go, too," I replied. "I've always gone!"

"I know. I wish you could go, too." The tears streamed

down her face. We embraced, and for the first time we cried it out together. Then, smiling through her tears, Mom whispered, "I feel better now."

"I do, too, Mom. I love you."

"I love you too, dear, although I'm not able to say all that I feel."

From that time forward Mom and I have known a special closeness, because we were at last able to be honest and open with each other about our true feelings.

Now, as I face the uncertainties of the future, I am constantly reminded of the depth of caring coming through from each member of my family.

Dad suffered a stroke and died very near the onset of my cancer battle. Dad, the one who worried over every chick in his brood, anxious that no harm should befall any of them. Word of his death reached me just as my own condition took a sudden turn for the worse. Somehow, it seemed good that he never knew of the crises that I must yet endure.

Simultaneously with our loss of Dad and with my turn for the worse, Mom—always our tiny monument of strength, our Rock of Gibraltar—fell and broke her hip. It was then, I guess, when I saw more than ever before the bond of oneness between each brother and sister. The phone lines buzzed across the nation as each kept the others in touch.

On one occasion when the family became aware of the sizable expenses that faced me, the total amount was paid in advance by anonymous donors. On another occasion one brother offered to give me his whole inheritance from Dad's estate. Others phoned often, sent cards and gifts. What a family! What God-given love! Precious above all were their words of encouragement and their prayers in my behalf. These were health-renewing gifts. Life was worth fighting for!

Aside from blood relatives were all my friends, acquaintances from near and far, and the church family. Unless you have gone through a similar experience, you can never realize the bond of fellowship that surfaces at such a time.

Constantly, beautiful flowers have arrived at unexpected

times, and with them came the smiling faces of those who delivered them and stayed for a while to chat. These flowers, thoughts, words, and gifts have meant so very much. Flowers at a funeral display beauty and thoughtfulness, but I have enjoyed these during life, and I like them this way best.

No expressions of gratitude can ever do justice to the labors of love from so many wonderful people. Many have freely spent countless hours in caring for my personal needs, in housecleaning, in making delicious foods. And again I think of my mother. At age 80, she should be enjoying every minute of her time in doing the relaxing things a retired person loves to do, but instead she has spent months with me, giving her time and energy to care for my needs—and with all the bounce of a 60-year-old.

Surely I must say with the psalmist, "I will sing of the mercies of the Lord for ever: with my mouth will I make known thy faithfulness to all generations" (Ps. 89:1). As Solomon said in Proverbs 16:24, "Pleasant words are as an honeycomb, sweet to the soul, and health to the bones."

The Big Crunch

No sooner had our eventful trip to the south ended when we headed once again for our yearly retreat in the redwoods. We had planned big for this year because we wanted both our mothers to share this year's campout with us.

My strength had ebbed, and the pain in my neck called for medication every four hours. The medication made me groggy and dull-thinking, but one thing came through loud and clear—we *were* going to the redwoods.

Mom advised against it. "You're not up to more travel just now. Let's stay home." But, no. I was bent on going, and go we did. Cec fixed up our camp in an ideal manner, as always. Conveniences were everywhere—clothesline, shelves, tables, canvas "rugs," even a makeshift shower (a five-gallon bucket overhead held water at whatever temperature we poured into it and a small hose provided a shower head).

Camping out again was invigorating. We joined our neighboring campers in fireside chats around the simple outdoor fireplace. Meetings were inspiring. I attended when I felt up to it and rested on the chaise lounge when the pain reached its peaks.

How many times had my battle with cancer interrupted these retreats? I'd about lost track, but it was great to be here, and I thanked God for the privilege.

One day, two days, passed. The grandmas prepared the meals, and on the first weekend friends joined us, bringing their food to add to ours. Sermons and music could be picked up over the radio, so much of the time I could enjoy the programs by air.

On Thursday morning of our second week, feeling a bit weak and finding that walking produced a slight tingle in my feet, I stepped from the van ever so carefully. Instantly, my right foot turned under, and I felt myself slumping to the ground. The fall was an easy, slow one, but I felt three pop! pop! pops! in my spine. Cec ran to help me up and eased me into a chair. At first, all seemed well. I felt no added pain. The rest of the day went quietly, and I kept my activity to a minimum. On Sabbath I listened to the services broadcast over the radio and enjoyed a good meal with family and fellow campers. Again, Mom's intuition felt that we should return home, but I wanted to stay for the last meeting, which would be that night.

Our conference president and his wife stopped by to see me and prayed with me before leaving. They also had a special prayer at the evening meeting—all of which touched my heart deeply. We enjoyed a final chat around the fire and settled down for a night's sleep prior to breaking up camp and heading home early the next morning.

At 3:00 A.M. I awakened, feeling the need to use our portable commode. Suddenly, I panicked. I had heard of people struck with paralysis, but surely this couldn't be in my case. When it dawned on me that I could not move a muscle, I became terrified. For two years I had lived a relatively normal, happy life, but now what? I could speak, so in panic I awoke Cec by gasping, "I can't move, Cec!"

His rude awakening shook him out of a sound slumber, and he helped me to the commode. Then I realized that my bladder would not function, and my abdomen was already distended. We cried for a while and prayed aloud for help from Heaven, then cried some more.

As dawn neared, Cec dressed, found the camp doctor—who gave orders for me to be admitted to the Ukiah Adventist Hospital—and then Cec went to work with a vengeance as he broke camp. The grandmothers helped desperately, and friends gathered to hasten us on our way.

In the van bed I was kept as comfortable as possible while Mom kept watch beside me. As I considered my life over that one hundred miles, I wondered whether this might be the last time that God could use my services. Hadn't I spent hours with other patients, some paralyzed and some in worse condition than mine? Hadn't I encouraged these people? Hadn't I spoken of God's love and healing power? Yet all at once I wondered where my own courage was. Where was my own faith that had carried me through the ups and downs of the past many months? Just as in my physical helplessness I had to let others care for me, so also I laid my helpless spiritual self in God's hands to do whatever He saw fit.

Before too long the nursing staff had settled me into a hospital bed and had shifted into high gear to relieve my immediate discomforts. I felt more relaxed now as my anxious husband spoon-fed me my evening meal. After I ate he helped me brush my teeth, for my hands were curled into tight claws—an impossible position for any functional use. My arms did move from the shoulder, and my elbows were free.

Early the next morning X-rays were taken, and then I had a session with a neurologist and with the orthopedic specialist who had first introduced me to the horrors of multiple myeloma.

After further tests, including a myelogram, they told me that the nerves had been pinched off at Number 5 in the cervical area of the spine.

The men advised me to consult a neurosurgeon in nearby Santa Rosa. Perhaps surgery might eliminate the pressure and restore mobility to the body. It was no sure thing, but there was at least hope for some restoration.

I arrived by ambulance later in the day. The neurosurgeon checked me over and scheduled surgery for the following day. Mom, Cec, and a friend stayed by me, but having been sedated, I recall very little of what happened from then on.

In my first moments of awareness following six hours of surgery, I could hear my husband praying aloud for me while my mother stood by, praying in her silent way.

I began to pray, too. "Lord, if this is it, and if I'm ready, let me go—let me sleep." Once again sleep folded me into her comfortable arms, but later I stirred and found that I was still breathing—though with much difficulty. I seemed to float in and out of consciousness—praying, recalling Bible promises, and slipping away into oblivion.

A text from Paul stood out clearly in my mind: "I have learned, in whatsoever state I am, therewith to be content" (Phil. 4:11). As I repeated it once, Cec bent over me and whispered, "Hang on to that one!"

When I became sufficiently conscious to learn of my condition, I was told that two and one-half vertebrae had been removed from my neck and were replaced with a meshwork of steel posts and wire, smoothed out with the type of "glue" used in total hip surgeries. A pulmonary specialist explained that my lungs had collapsed and only by fighting to reinflate the lungs, fighting for life itself, would I be able to make it.

Was it worth the fight? Why not let go now? Again I asked God to allow me to let go if He saw fit, and again I closed my eyes and drifted off into nothingness, but not for long.

Awake again, I cried, "Lord! Why am I still here?" But the fact remained that I was still here. I had frequently questioned whether I could be of any more use. Here I lay absolutely helpless, without the use of hands or feet. However, I could hear and I could speak. I asked the Lord what He wanted me to do with my limited abilities. But even then I felt as if I wanted just to go to sleep and forget it all. As the pastor visited me one day, I angrily said to him, "God doesn't need me to finish His work. He doesn't even need you! Yet it has been a privilege to participate in it. I would like to continue to be a part of it. Pastor, how can I possibly be of any use in this condition?"

His eyes dropped. He looked at the floor. There seemed to be no answer, but he said, "The Lord has a work for you, too. We don't know what it is, but He will reveal it in due time."

I decided that I must talk to the radiologists and oncologists who had administered my radiation. I knew that I should resume the treatments almost immediately. The doctor came and I asked him if he felt the fight was worth it, knowing the end result of myeloma. He listened carefully, then answered: "You have a right to choose to let go, but, Evie, I certainly don't ever like to quit a job before I've done all I can—and I haven't done all I can yet."

That was the spark I needed, and the answer Heaven had for me! We would fight to pull through this crisis, and with God's power would come through to glorify His name. Meanwhile, I would ask constantly to learn to be content in whatever state I found myself.

Suddenly, activity resumed before I felt capable of handling it. Every four hours around the clock the respiratory therapists awakened me and required me to breathe deeply into a machine. They also vibrated my chest area to dislodge mucus in the lungs. I would cough violently; it was important in order to extricate the fluid. But it was very painful. By firmly pushing on my abdomen they forced me to cough over and over again. They taught Cecil how to push so I would cough. These occasions seemed almost constant until, completely exhausted, I would fall asleep—only to awaken engulfed in another gasp of coughing up phlegm. Daily trips by ambulance to the radiation center also became part of the busy schedule I felt so unable to meet.

After five days in the Intensive Care Unit, I was transferred to a room on the main nursing floor. Nurses moved in with constant, loving care, as they had always done in ICU.

Still praying consciously and subconsciously as I drifted in and out of the medication's influence, I little realized the listening ears who heard my conversations with Heaven. Later the nurses would slip in beside me and ask about these conversations, and I could tell them about the marvelous power of God and explain how prayer played such an important role in my life. "You're surely receiving grace from somewhere," one nurse said in amazement as she slipped away from my bedside. And, oh, how true it was! The comfort, the peace, that held me close to Him hour after hour and day after day!

My first night in a regular patient room was long and very wearing. About 9:00 P.M. I began a series of coughs that suctioned huge amounts of phlegm. Cec jumped to his feet beside me, pressing my abdomen to aid the coughing. For six long hours we worked together until I felt totally exhausted, and he slumped wearily back into his chair. The crisis had ended. Though I endured many more heavy coughing spells, none were as long and grueling as this one.

Friends came to relieve Cec at night and stayed with me around the clock for two weeks. Blessed angels from heaven, these! To stand by so faithfully, so full of love, so giving!

Little by little, strength began to take hold. Hour after hour the respiratory therapists stopped by to administer further treatment. They always had a smile and a happy, cheerful attitude. How good is God, I thought. How merciful! How He works through so many of His people to sustain life when it is nearly gone.

By now I had begun to wonder about my neck—a metal neck! Did I dare turn my head? Would it squeak? I finally managed the courage to twist my head, and it moved with ease—no squeaks. But even earlier, when I was to receive radiation for that very area, a great fear had arisen in my mind. With all that glue and metal, would the powerful treatment of radiation do something to my neck? Perhaps the glue would crack and disintegrate! I decided that no technician would touch my neck unless I first spoke to Dr. S—despite my weakened condition and all the paraphernalia for IVs and oxygen around. He listened attentively while I spilled out my fears and seriously assured me that there would be no problem. He may have chuckled all the way back to his office, but I appreciated his allowing me to express my fears and his simple explanations that allayed my fears.

The days passed. Just as I began to feel like eating again, a yeast infection took hold in my mouth, then a radiation burn added to the pain in my throat. I was miserable. Unable to eat any but soft foods, I lost weight. The dietitians tempted me with extra foods, but to no avail until at last the infection subsided, and the treatments for both problems began to show results.

Little by little my strength returned under the loving care of dedicated doctors and nurses. Finally, the day came when I began to hear suggestions of possibly going home soon.

During this time our little family had come from Iowa to help, and their daily visits worked like medicine. I could hardly wait to spend more time at home with them. Les and our two little grandsons could not stay long enough for that, but Beth and 3-year-old Allison stayed. Beth cleaned the house, came sixty miles to visit me, and even gave her life's blood when I needed it. And I fought hard to get well enough to return home while they at least were still with us.

The physicians and nurses prepared Cec and me ever so carefully for the transition. One day the doctor sat down beside me and earnestly explained that if Cec could learn to handle some careful nursing techniques I could go directly home. Otherwise it would be better for me to transfer to the hospital in Ukiah. Cec, having worked in a hospital atmosphere for some twenty-five years, rallied well and passed all the tests expected of him. Soon the plans gelled for my departure from the hospital.

Again the caring doctor sat beside me to prepare me for my part. "You must realize," he explained, "that you face the possibility of being paraplegic for life, and this will be a rough adjustment. But the adjustment will be equally as difficult for Cecil, and you must be prepared for this."

By this time I could move my arms and hands a little. With the aid of a hand device I could feed myself and brush my teeth, although I could not use a pen or comb or anything small, owing to the rigidity of my fingers. However, each day I exercised them carefully, and the movement was improving. I still had no movement in my feet at all, and no movement in the legs or toes.

The final day came. I could go home. A month had gone by since surgery. Loving nurses came to bid me goodbye. Tears flowed as gratitude for their loving care welled up deep inside me. Our van awaited my entry. This time, I rode on a gurney out to the waiting vehicle. The male nurses and a couple of ambulance men helped Cec load me in, and we headed for home!

Home! I had hardly been there since June 29, when we had left for Mexico. An hour and a half later we pulled into the driveway, and there across the front of the house hung a banner that read, "Welcome Home, Evie!" A big, yellow ribbon decorated the front juniper tree. The pure-white curtains wafted gently in the breeze, displaying a fresh laundry job done with the loving hands of a daughter.

I noticed dozens of notes on the banner, all were written by friends from the local home hospital. Notes of welcome. Notes of love. Suddenly, from somewhere, I felt a lump in my throat!

Inside, a hospital bed awaited my occupancy, right in the living room, where all the action occurs. It all looked so good. Home! What a thrill! Yet I felt so very weary. Cecil quickly tucked me into bed, while Beth prepared a delicious meal. Ah, how good is our God! How marvelous are His ways! Thank You, God, for home. Thank You, God, for family and for friends—and I dozed off for a dream or two before dinner.

Learning Through Help of Professionals

"Push, Evie, push!" The voice of my physical therapist commanded gently but firmly. I pushed as best as my wasted leg would push—a weak attempt to say the least. "Now more, a little more." Perspiration beaded my brow as I tried again, and still he wanted more!

Suddenly his black face broke into a grin. "Good! Now you're doing it!" The exercise continued, every stroke an extreme effort. My mind wandered a bit to a distraction at the window. "You're not with me, Evie!" he barked.

"How do you know? I'm still exercising with you."

"Yes, but the mind and muscle must work together and your mind wandered—I could tell it in your muscle response!" I marveled as my mind got back to business. This was more than fun. It was work. From one area of the body to another Herman worked, instructing me carefully until at last the end of the session left me exhausted.

In later sessions he repeated some of the same exercises and then added a few more difficult procedures until, frightened, I found myself learning, like a tiny child, to sit up and dangle my feet over the edge of the bed. The floor seemed so far down, and my fear of falling was acute, yet Herman steadily guided, urged, and watched. Little by little I began to trust him.

It reminded me all over again of learning to trust God, step by step, in areas where I could not see ahead. It was as though He said to me, "Now, here's a human example of what I'm trying to teach you. He will not let you down. You can see him, and you are learning to believe he will keep you from falling.

Now, child, you may trust Me even more. I will never leave you, and I will keep you from falling."

Eventually, treatments advanced to the point that additional sessions were ordered for me, not only with Herman, at home, but now in the pool at the hospital's physical-therapy department. Here, Christie took over. She was a quiet, almost bashful girl, who said little, smiled much, and knew her therapy business well.

I had seen the pool many times, since my husband had helped design and install the equipment. A stretcher hung ominously overhead. Christie lowered it to a position where I could be transferred onto it, then gently it soared again into mid-air, moving steadily to a position over the pool of water.

I felt my conveyance lowering and I wanted to grab something to keep from falling, yet Christie took such care in moving the stretcher that my fear soon subsided. Down and down I went until I touched the water, and oh, how good it felt! With a life jacket on, I floated off the stretcher into the pool. Freedom! Water! Beautiful! It had been months since my body had been immersed in water. This was such a relaxing experience, I knew I could stay here for hours.

But, no. Again there was work to do. Christie set about showing me leg movements to practice as well as other exercises. Soon my strength waned and the trip out of the tank became a welcome one.

Day after day I worked out, sometimes treading water. This was extremely difficult since my legs seemed almost a separated part of me, yet in time the task did become a bit easier.

Eventually it came time for me to try standing at the parallel bars, having graduated from the water. Frightened at having to rely on my weak legs, I broke out in perspiration. But Christie was there, ready always to protect me. At times, another therapist and Cec also aided, and one day, with their support, I took twenty steps. As difficult as it was, my courage seized onto the hope that I might walk before many months—barring any further incidence of myeloma cells in the bone.

LEARNING THROUGH HELP OF PROFESSIONALS

Each day I gained more and more respect for the value of physical therapy. The faithful teamwork of these dedicated therapists had greatly helped my recovery. I asked Christie what physical therapy really meant to her. She explained it to me in terms of her training: "Physical therapy is a health-care profession whose primary purpose is to aid in rehabilitation. Physical therapists evaluate neuromuscular, musculo-skeletal, sensorimotor and related cardiovascular and respiratory functions of the patients. They plan and implement initial and subsequent programs based on their findings within the referral of a licensed M.D.

"Utilization of such agents as heat, water, electricity, exercise, light, and massage are used in treating patients.

"Appropriate psychological and sociological principles are applied in motivating and instructing the patient, family, and others. All aspects of the patient's well-being are taken into consideration. The end result is ultimately up to the patient. The desire to attain the set goals for self-improvement is of great importance to the outcome of the treatments. As goals are met, new and higher goals are set.

"Physical therapy is a field in which we help the patient help himself through education and a large variety of techniques available to us."

The workouts, then, were more than just exercises. Each movement counted for something. There was a muscle or a set of muscles to activate that tied in with my specific need.

Truly the body is fearfully and wonderfully made. Our Creator has built in it amazing reconstructive abilities that we can use in cooperation with His healing power. Sometimes Herman insisted on my singing with him, and even that was designed to develop my weakened lungs. Not a wasted movement. My admiration and respect for the value of this God-given art and the ones He had called into this service were profound. As I thought gratefully of the good received in such cheerful manner, I remembered other physical therapists who had bent over me, patiently working through some early stages of my paralysis while I spent the long month in the hospital.

My mind then wandered to the respiratory therapists who had spent hours working with me to restore the collapsed lung. I thought of the occupational therapist who had cheerfully made a device to fit my hand so that I could hold a spoon.

The picture enlarged as I recalled the many loving nurses who did all they could to encourage me and to make my discomforts bearable. One kind nurse vividly stood out in my mind's eye. I could still see her bending over me so very soon after surgery and reading a poem that touched my heart deeply. The poem depicted a God who knew as no one else could know just what I was experiencing at that very moment. Then there was the nurse who slipped softly to my bedside in ICU and asked me from where my strength came. "You seem so full of grace!" she breathed. I assured her that my Lord was the only answer. He provided strength for each need. She slipped thoughtfully and quietly away. I thanked Heaven for all these angels of mercy who had so faithfully stood by my side.

The sense of gratitude within enlarged as I reminisced about the many doctors who had treated me. Some were personal friends; others were specialists in certain fields. Again my gratitude soared for my personal friend and family doctor, who must have had a difficult time breaking the final word to me of my diagnosis. It almost seemed as though his hair had grown a shade grayer this past year or two. Did my condition help put one or two of those gray hairs there?

Again, in review, I remembered the orthopedic doctor's words when he first explained the nature of myeloma. I thought of the oncologist, who seemed upset when he had to answer "I don't know" to my pointed questions regarding my future possibilities. At first I had thought, He doesn't really care! Yet now, after having dealt with the various men of medicine for four years, I knew that each one cared very deeply and would have done anything within his power to have helped me if it had been possible.

The medical center where I received radiation therapy, with its lilting, pervasive music over the intercom, also held happy memories for me. The staff members dealt with all of us on a pleasant, first-name basis. They must have had a pep talk daily to keep so cheerful! Despite the morbidity of working constantly with cancer patients, the personnel constantly chuckled and teased a bit, always, always happy. How could a patient leave depressed under such conditions?

I would like to be able to say that as I write these words all my muscles function normally again, but that is not true as yet. Movement in my arms and hands has returned. My feet and legs moved not at all until two and one-half months after surgery, when one evening a faint movement showed in my toes. Cecil had so constantly hoped and trusted that they would regain movement that he would say each day, "Let's see you move your toes."

I became so weary of even thinking it could happen that when he repeated his request one evening inwardly I wanted to lash out and kick. In fact, impulsively I went through the mental gymnastics of doing just that in a fit of inward anger. Suddenly, Cec jumped. "You did it! They moved!" He ran to Mom's bedroom and called for her to come and see. Yes, my toes moved, and soon my feet moved. Later the legs showed signs of action. The physical therapist subsequently went to work with renewed zeal, bringing more muscles into cooperation.

The ability to stand up and take a few steps has so far been the extent of my recovery. The future remains uncertain. But I am confident that God's grace will supply the power and the healing as I continue to cooperate with the forces He has provided.

Meanwhile, my gratitude overflows when I reflect on His leading, particularly during these eight months of paralysis.

Home at Last!

The end of the story has come, because time has caught up with the present.

I do not know the future, but I do know that today is here and tomorrow has not yet come. Today has come—to be lived to the fullest. I shall laugh, sing a bit, and praise Him for this one more day.

It's still very possible that He could work a miracle that would restore my health. How often I've dreamed of that possibility and would love to participate in such a tremendously exciting event! How thrilling it must have been to be the crippled man whom Jesus restored when He walked this earth—to have leaped up on legs made strong and to have run to share with everyone what the Lord had done for him!

Yet, our heavenly Father has not promised miracles for all of us. I must trust that in His wisdom and knowledge He knows whether a sudden miracle in my case would honor Him. I must trust Him with the answer. My interest is sharply focused upon heaven and the lovely Jesus who will greet us on the resurrection day—and I can hardly wait for that day.

As I came out from the anesthetic following the long surgery, scenes came and went before my unconscious eyes. One scene I remember vividly, brief though it was. It seemed that I had died and had been buried in the earth. Time meant nothing to me, but my first conscious moment came as the ground around me seemed to be moving. I suddenly realized that it was an earthquake—*the* earthquake! I shook myself and looked up. And there, as I surfaced above ground, I heard a mighty trumpet sounding and a musical but powerful voice shouting, "Awake! Awake!" It was Jesus! There He was in far more splendor than I had ever imagined. People were singing. Angels were singing. Some angels were flying to the people rising from the graves. This was it; this was homecoming!

As exciting as it had been for me to return home from my long hospital stay, that thrill held no comparison to the one visualized so realistically that day when the Lord allowed me in my hour of need to catch a glimpse of what He has in store for us.

And I know it's true, because 1 Thessalonians 4:16, 17 describes it: "For the Lord himself shall descend from heaven with a shout, with the voice of the archangel, and with the trump of God: and the dead in Christ shall rise first: then we which are alive and remain shall be caught up together with them in the clouds, to meet the Lord in the air: and so shall we ever be with the Lord."

And also: "In a moment, in the twinkling of an eye, at the last trump: for the trumpet shall sound, and the dead shall be raised incorruptible, and we shall be changed" (1 Cor. 15:52).

How I thank Him for that preview! How I long to see that day! Will I be alive when Jesus comes? Will I sleep for a while first? Does it really matter, when He knows the end from the beginning, and we can trust Him completely?

Our lifespan on this earth is such a tiny moment compared to the forever in eternity. There "God shall wipe away all tears from their eyes; and there shall be no more death, neither sorrow, nor crying, neither shall there be any more pain" (Rev. 21:4).

That homecoming reunion will surpass any we've ever enjoyed here. There we must meet—with no places left vacant. And should it be His will that I should rest for a while—do you care enough for me to allow me that rest through the last events?

Can you love enough to let me go and not have feelings of guilt that you "should have done this or that for her" or "should have been there"?

Do you love enough to let things remain in His hands and to

begin more than ever to center your attention upon the loving Jesus and the plans He has made for our great homecoming?

Meet me there!

Appendix

MR. TENTMAKER

It was nice living in this tent when it was strong and secure and the sun was shining and the air was warm.

But, Mr. Tentmaker, it's scary now.

My tent is acting like it's not going to hold together. The poles seem weak, and they shift with the wind. A couple of the stakes have wiggled loose from the sand, and, worst of all, the canvas has a rip. It no longer protects me from beating rain or stinging flies.

It's scary in here, Mr. Tentmaker. Last week I was sent to the repair shop and some repairmen tried to patch the rip in my canvas. It didn't help much though, because the patch pulled away from the edges, and now the tear is worse.

What troubled me most, Mr. Tentmaker, is that the repairmen didn't seem to notice that I was still in the tent. They just worked on the canvas while I shivered inside. I cried out once, but no one heard me.

I guess my first real question is, Why did You give me such a flimsy tent? I can see by looking around the campground that some of the tents are much stronger and more stable than mine. Why, Mr. Tentmaker, did You pick a tent of such poor quality for me and even more important, what do You intend to do about it?

Oh, little tent dweller, as the Creator and Provider of tents, I know all about you and your tent, and I love you both.

I made a tent for myself once and lived in it on your campground. My tent was vulnerable, too, and some vicious attackers ripped it to pieces while I was still in it. It was a terrible experience, but you'll be glad to know they couldn't hurt Me. In fact, the whole occurrence was a tremendous advantage, because it is this very victory over My enemy that frees Me to be of present help to you.

Little tent dweller, I am now prepared to come and live in your tent with you, if you will invite Me. You will learn as we dwell together that real security comes from My being in your tent with you. When the storms come, you can huddle in My arms and I'll hold you. When the canvas rips, we'll go to the repair shop together.

Someday, little tent dweller, your tent will collapse (for I've only designed it for temporary use). But I promise not to leave before you do. Later I will provide you with a new tent—one that will last forever. And you may pitch it in My eternal campground.

Anonymous

FAVORITE TEXTS AND QUOTES

"I will never leave thee, nor forsake thee" (Heb. 13:5).

"The Lord is my shepherd; I shall not want. He maketh me to lie down in green pastures: he leadeth me beside the still waters. He restoreth my soul: he leadeth me in the paths of righteousness for his name's sake. Yea, though I walk through the valley of the shadow of death, I will fear no evil: for thou art with me; thy rod and thy staff they comfort me. Thou preparest a table before me in the presence of mine enemies: thou anointest my head with oil; my cup runneth over. Surely goodness and mercy shall follow me all the days of my life: and I will dwell in the house of the Lord for ever" (Ps. 23).

"Thou wilt keep him in perfect peace, whose mind is stayed on thee: because he trusteth in thee" (Isa. 26:3).

"For I have learned, in whatsoever state I am, therewith to be content" (Phil. 4:11).

"There hath no temptation taken you but such as is common to man: but God is faithful, who will not suffer you to be tempted above that ye are able; but will with the temptation also make a way of escape, that ye may be able to bear it" (1 Cor. 10:13).

"For ever, O Lord, thy word is settled in heaven" (Ps. 119:89).

"Great peace have they which love thy law: and nothing shall offend them" (Ps. 119:165).

"Oh that men would praise the Lord for his goodness, and for his wonderful works to the children of men! " (Ps. 107:21).

"Open thou mine eyes, that I may behold wondrous things out of thy law" (Ps. 119:18).

"I am the vine, ye are the branches: He that abideth in me, and I in him, the same bringeth forth much fruit: for without me ye can do nothing" (John 15:5).

"My brethren, count it all joy when ye fall into divers temptations [trials]; knowing this, that the trying of your faith worketh patience"(James 1:2, 3).

"Because thou hast kept the word of my patience, I also will keep thee from the hour of temptation [trial], which shall come upon all the world, to try them that dwell upon the earth" (Rev. 3:10).

"All that the Father giveth me shall come to me; and him that cometh to me I will in no wise cast out" (John 6:37).

"According to the eternal purpose which he purposed in Christ Jesus our Lord" (Eph. 3:11).

"The will of God will never lead you where the grace of God cannot keep you."—Anonymous.

"With nations, with families, and with individuals, He has often permitted matters to come to a crisis, that His interference might become marked."—*Positive Christian Living,* p. 156.

"If we keep the Lord ever before us, allowing our hearts to go out in thanksgiving and praise to Him, we shall have a continual freshness in our religious life. Our prayers will take the form of conversation with God as we would talk with a friend. He will speak His mysteries to us personally."—*Ibid.,* p. 110.

"Circumstances have but little to do with the experiences of the soul. It is the spirit cherished which gives coloring to all our actions. A man at peace with God and his fellow men cannot be made miserable."—*Testimonies,* vol. 5, p. 488.

"We love our Lord to the extent we love the person we like the least."—Anonymous.

"Those who bring their petitions to God, claiming His promise while they do not comply with the conditions, insult Jehovah."—*Positive Christian Living,* p. 119.

"He has always chosen extremities, when there seemed no possible chance for deliverance from Satan's workings, for the manifestation of His power. Man's necessity is God's opportunity."—*Testimonies,* vol. 5, p. 714.

Epilogue

Soon after Evelyn completed the manuscript for *On My Back, Looking Up!* she broke her hip. X-rays revealed that cancer had honeycombed her legs and back. The physicians wondered how she had lived as long as she had in such an advanced diseased condition. There was little they could do for her but suggest another round of radiation treatments. For a year Evelyn lay on her back at home. Cecil turned the back porch into a solarium, where she could soak up as much sunshine as possible. Finally, he quit his job so he could totally devote himself to her care.

Even during this difficult time Evelyn was a source of encouragement to many. Friends streamed in and out of her room—and left with a lighter step and a more buoyant spirit. Evelyn fretted over her book. If a publisher did not accept it, how could she continue to tell others about God's loving care once she had gone?

Early in December, 1982, Evelyn came down with pneumonia. Cecil rushed her to the hospital. "Let's give it all we can," she urged the doctors. After her first day of hospitalization, she lost her voice. Friends volunteered to stay by her side and helped while away the hours by reading the Bible to her.

On the third day, Evelyn slipped into a coma. Friends continued their vigil and continued to read the Scriptures aloud. Apparently their voices penetrated her consciousness, for as long as they kept reading God's Word she would lie there calmly. Whenever they stopped, Evelyn would show signs of restlessness.

The next day—December 7—Evelyn died. The night before, three visitors had opened their hearts to Christ while they hovered near her. Evelyn's dedicated life continued to influence others even as she lay on her deathbed. Monday, December 13, nearly five hundred people—from many walks of life and denominations—paid their last respects at her funeral.

Evelyn no longer suffers the terrible ravages of multiple myeloma, but her testimony to God's tender care lives on in the pages of her book.